WHAT PEOPLE SAY ABOUT

Preparing Witnesses To Give Effective Testimony

Preparing Witnesses to Give Effective Testimony *is an invaluable handbook of lessons culled from thousands of witness preparation sessions, and it functions both as a great primer for new attorneys about to prepare their first witness and as a qualified refresher for the seasoned litigator. The book's pointers are practical and effective, and they will improve the testimony of even the most challenging witness. As I read it, I found myself scribbling notes on my next witness preparation outline. I hope opposing counsel never finds this book.*

PETER B. MOORES, PARTNER
Choate, Hall & Stewart LLP, Boston, MA

One of a trial attorney's most difficult, poorly executed, and outright neglected tasks is witness preparation. It's also one of the most important. Preparing Witnesses to Give Effective Testimony *guides you away from the blunders—such as all that "Don't say this! Don't do that!" advice, which can sink the ship. In clear terms Dodge and Ryan cover why witness preparation is difficult, why you must not neglect it, and their approach to solving its difficulties.*

DAVID BALL, PH.D.
Nationally known trial and jury consultant
Malekpour Oliver Ball Research & Consulting
Author of *David Ball on Damages* and co-author of *Reptile*

Dodge and Ryan have done a nice job of condensing knowledge about preparing witnesses into this handy guide. They are especially effective at distinguishing between what witnesses need for depositions versus trials. I like their presentations of "safe harbor" answers, of how to address performance anxiety in witnesses, and how to keep the expectations realistic when preparing witnesses. This book can serve as a thoughtful, how-to-do-it aid for attorneys who seek to spend their time well in the preparation of credible witnesses.

STANLEY L. BRODSKY, PH.D.
Professor, Department of Psychology and
Director, Witness Research Lab
The University of Alabama
Author of *The Expert Expert Witness* and nine other books

Angela and John's years of hands-on experience offer trial attorneys insight to understand their client's personality, concerns, and communication nuances. It empowers the [trial] team to guide the [client] on how to testify their truth in a personable, confident, and convincing manner. Guidelines on how to avoid pitfalls are effectively addressed. [The authors] present effective ground work for educating clients to the process, how to provide support, and how to establish a trust and comfort level that will benefit the client and the case. We are huge advocates of preparing witnesses for deposition and trial and this book presents the "how to" in an engaging and useful way.

ERIC HOLM
Vice President of Claims
Physicians Insurance: A Mutual Company

Preparing Witnesses to Give Effective Testimony

The Attorney's Essential Guide

Angela M. Dodge, Ph.D. and John H. Ryan, Ph.D.
Litigation Psychologists

Dodge Consulting & Publications, LLP

The material contained herein represents the opinions, views and professional experience of the authors, and should not be construed to be the views or opinions of the law firms or companies with whom the authors are associated or to whom the authors have provided consulting services.

Nothing contained in this handbook is to be considered as the rendering of legal advice. Readers are responsible for obtaining such advice from their own legal counsel. This handbook and any checklists or forms herein are intended for educational and informational purposes only. The authors are litigation psychologists, and have no formal legal training, nor are they licensed to practice law in any state.

Dodge Consulting & Publications, LLP
14591 Wiley Lane SE
Olalla, WA 98359
(253) 857-7716
adodge@dodgeconsulting.com or jryan@dodgeconsulting.com

For more information about publications available through
Dodge Consulting & Publications LLP, please visit the website at
www.dodgepublications.com

Cover and text design by Kathy Campbell
Edited by Barbara Fandrich

Printed by Gorham Printing, Washington State
Printed in the United States of America
First Printing: April 2013
ISBN 978-0-9777511-6-7

DEDICATION

This handbook is dedicated to the late
Margaret Fahn, a genius at interrogating witnesses
to a variety of childhood crimes, including
broken dishes, muddy dresses, and
suspicious-looking household pets.

Other books available from Dodge Consulting & Publications LLP

Handbook for Witnesses: A Guide for Testifying at a Deposition, Hearing, or Trial by Angela M. Dodge, Ph.D. and John H. Ryan, Ph.D. (Print Date: May 2013). Available by contacting adodge@dodgeconsulting.com or at www.amazon.com after May 2013.

ISBN: 978-0-9777511-9-8 ($19.95 plus S&H).

When Good Doctors Get Sued: A Practical Guide for Physicians Involved in Malpractice Lawsuits by Angela M. Dodge, Ph.D. in collaboration with Steven F. Fitzer, J.D. (Third Printing, 2009). Available by contacting adodge@dodgeconsulting.com or at www.amazon.com.

ISBN: 978-09777511-0-5 ($24.95 plus S&H).

Opening Statements–Closing Arguments by Ronald J. Matlon, Ph.D. (Second Edition, 2009) Available through www.dodgepublications.com or at www.amazon.com.

ISBN: 978-0-9777511-3-6 ($19.95 plus S&H).

Winning at Jury Selection: A Handbook of Practical Jury-Focused Techniques & Strategies by Angela M. Dodge, Ph.D. (July, 2010). Available by contacting adodge@dodgeconsulting.com or at www.amazon.com.

ISBN: 978-09777511-4-3 ($34.95 plus S&H).

CONTENTS

ACKNOWLEDGMENTS

We wish to express deep appreciation and gratitude to the thousands of witnesses who have challenged and developed our skills, and the hundreds of outstanding attorneys with whom we have worked. You have taught us much over the years, and we hope we have reflected it adequately in these pages. Special thanks to Barbara Fandrich, our editor, who made this a much better book in so many ways. We are grateful for your contribution. Thanks also to Peter Moores, a talented attorney who practices in Boston, MA, for his insightful comments on chapter sequencing. His advice made a difference, and we are grateful for the time he devoted to a thoughtful reading of the manuscript.

We are also indebted to our colleagues, the many professional litigation consultants with whom we have interacted at conferences, meetings, and workshops, and whose ideas have influenced our own practices. We hope they feel honored to see their impact reflected in this book.

The phrase "effective truth-telling" belongs to Steven Fitzer, personal friend and senior partner at Fitzer, Leighton & Ayers LLP in Tacoma, WA. It is a brilliant characterization and we hope he is pleased that we have adopted it. He will also undoubtedly see his influence reflected throughout this book.

The "Rule of 3" referred to in Chapter 6 is borrowed from John Graffe, a senior partner at Johnson, Graffe, Keay, Moniz & Wick LLP, a premier law firm based in Seattle, WA. John has provided us with many opportunities to hone our skills, and with a variety of colorful phrases and helpful analogies to use in preparation sessions.

The phrases “staying inside your box” and “train wreck versus an auto accident” were first heard from Brian Rekofke, an accomplished attorney and partner at Witherspoon Kelley in Spokane, WA. These phrases will make more sense when you read them in this book. They made immediate sense to us when we heard them. Thanks, Brian.

INTRODUCTION

What is effective witness testimony? Attorneys present their cases through evidence and witnesses. The evidence usually speaks for itself. But how well will your witnesses speak for the facts? How convincing and believable will they be? How truthful will they appear to the triers of fact? How effective? How influential and persuasive? How impressive? How can an attorney get maximum value from the time s/he will spend preparing witnesses to give credible and effective testimony at a deposition, hearing or trial? These are some of the key questions this handbook addresses.

Most trial attorneys will find themselves in court much less often than in a conference room conducting the deposition of a witness, defending a witness in a deposition, or preparing a witness for a legal or investigative forum. The ability to prepare a witness effectively is perhaps the most important and frequently used skill a trial attorney can possess. In fact, an integral part of the attorney's discovery and trial preparation process is to actively participate in the preparation of witnesses. While conducting a deposition or trial examination is a critical element of legal training, skill in evaluating and preparing witnesses from a communications standpoint is often a neglected aspect of their education. Most new attorneys acquire witness preparation experience and skills by "trial and error" or observing more senior members of the law practice.

This book is intended to develop attorney skills in this critical aspect of an attorney's practice, and to expand and hone the skills of experienced litigators. It is based on several decades of trial consulting practice with thousands of witnesses from all walks of life, occupations, professions, and levels of communication skill, and on our experience with many different kinds of cases, both civil and criminal.

This handbook for attorneys is intended to be accompanied by the *Handbook for Witnesses*. The witness handbook is a resource for witnesses, to be used as a refresher of advice and guidance they have been given in a preparation session. It can also be a substitute when formal preparation is not available to them. It is highly recommended that attorneys make this resource available to their witnesses. (See Appendix C for ordering information.)

The Experience of the Authors

Over the course of our careers, we have worked with thousands of witnesses and their attorneys, conducted scores of post-trial interviews with actual jurors, and carried out hundreds of pre-trial focus groups in which we have asked mock jurors for their reactions to segments of witness testimony. Hundreds of deposition transcripts and video recordings have been read and critiqued. This extensive experience has taught us:

1. Some witnesses are better than others because they are simply more effective truth tellers.
2. All witnesses can be improved—some more than others.
3. Jurors and judges gauge the credibility of witnesses not only on the basis of *what* the witness says, but also on *how* it is expressed.
4. One of the most serious errors made by attorneys is misjudging the impact of a witness's testimony on jurors or judges.
5. The best witnesses are those who have been carefully prepared to be effective communicators in a legal setting.

6. In witness preparation, one size does not fit all. Every witness is unique, and each preparation session must be uniquely tailored to a witness's concerns, needs, strengths, and communication skills.

Much of the advice we have given attorneys and witnesses in witness preparation and trial strategy sessions is applicable whether:

- Preparing a person for deposition, trial, hearing, or board of inquiry
- A witness is testifying on behalf of the plaintiff, the prosecution, the defense, the petitioner, the respondent, or the court
- The person is a party in the case, an expert witness, or a fact witness
- The person is young or elderly, savvy about the legal process or naïve, well-educated or not, confident or simply frightened out of their wits

What we have learned from attorneys and witnesses in over twenty years of experience is that legal counselors who fail to adequately prepare their witnesses have significantly weakened their cases before they ever enter the courtroom. Effective witness testimony is the cornerstone of trial strategy and outcome because attorneys don't win or lose cases, witnesses and evidence usually do.

The Benefits of Reading This Book

This book is designed to build the skills of both new and experienced attorneys so they can better prepare their witnesses and individualize their preparation sessions. Chapters deal with:

- Understanding what it means to be an effective witness and why this is so critical to your case (Chapter 1)

- Becoming more sensitive to the witness's perspective and needs, which builds rapport and trust between witness and attorney (Chapters 2 and 10)
- Establishing concrete goals for witness preparation based on the individual needs of the witness and of counsel (Chapter 3)
- Assessing the witness's communication strengths and challenges so the preparation can be focused, efficient, effective, and tailored to the individual witness (Chapter 4)
- Managing expectations about what can be accomplished in preparation sessions, based on your assessment of the witness's needs (Chapter 5)
- Educating witnesses to their role, the expectations of counsel, and how their testimony fits into counsel's overall case strategy (Chapter 6)
- Providing specific steps and techniques to prepare witnesses to give the most effective and influential testimony possible (Chapter 7)
- Helping witnesses to refresh their memories and recall events more accurately (Chapter 8)
- Addressing several special witness challenges (Chapter 9)
- Dealing with emotional issues (Chapter 10)
- Discussing issues surrounding the discoverability of witness preparation (Chapter 11)

Reading This Book May Not Be Enough

Attorneys are trained to focus on *facts* and the organization of facts, testimony, and evidence into a coherent case to be presented to a panel of fact-finders. They are less well-trained in *how* witness testimony is best presented to jurors, judges, mediators, and others who will assess the credibility and truthfulness of that testimony.

Most attorneys believe the facts will speak for themselves. In reality, the facts often must be spoken through the voices of witnesses—and the impact of the voices of witnesses is often misjudged. Witnesses expected to be persuasive on the stand fall apart, witnesses thought to be articulate and informative end up confusing jurors and losing the potential for influence, witnesses known to have considerable litigation experience are discounted by jurors who see them as "hired guns" because their answers appear scripted or coached.

The misjudging of a witness's ability and potential impact is what we call the "attorney blind spot." One of the most important roles a trial consultant or litigation psychologist can play in the litigation process is witness impact assessment. An honest and objective assessment of a witness by a professional who has no stake in the outcome of a trial or hearing is one of the most value-added services an attorney can obtain. If the reading of this book leaves you with the feeling that a trial consultant is still needed, there should be no hesitation to call on one. (See Chapter 10 for suggestions on how to find a consultant in your area.)

CHAPTER 1

Why Witness Preparation Is Critical to Your Case

One of the most persuasive components of evidence in any case is the source that presents it. Most jurors, because of their own background and life experiences, are predisposed to trust some witnesses and not others. In a courtroom, jurors must rely on rather quick judgments and verbal and behavioral cues to determine who is trustworthy—who is believable. Therefore, it is critical to create positive first impressions of your client, your fact witnesses, your expert witnesses, and yourself in order for jurors to believe your evidence and your case over that of the opposition. If your witnesses are unable to create a positive, credible impression with jurors, your sound evidence and brilliant arguments will be defeated. A key to winning your case is to avoid putting on the stand any witness who is not prepared to give effective, truthful, and persuasive testimony.

What It Means to Be an Effective Witness

"Effective" testimony means speaking in a way that influences jurors positively. To be effective, a witness must impact jurors in five important ways:

1. Jurors must HEAR what the witness has to say. Most jurors first listen with their "gut instinct." If the testimony does not connect with them at a visceral or intuitive level, it does not get processed at the cognitive level. Then the juror is likely to "not hear" it, disregard it, or discount it. This means the testimony does not get registered at the cognitive or understanding level. Also, for jurors to hear testimony accurately, the volume of speech must be high enough so even the juror in the farthest seat can hear clearly, and information must be conveyed in a way that prompts jurors to listen carefully.

2. Jurors must UNDERSTAND the answers given by witnesses to the questions posed. This means the witness must be able to articulate information and thoughts in a way that is lucid and comprehensible. For example, a witness who speaks too rapidly or slowly, has a pronounced accent, gives long and tangential lectures, uses professional jargon not familiar to jurors, mumbles, or otherwise lacks clarity of speech will not be effective.

3. It is critical that jurors BELIEVE the witness's testimony, especially when it conflicts with other evidence or testimony. How are jurors to determine who is telling the truth? Typically, they use a variety of auditory and body language cues to judge the veracity of each witness, and once they decide a witness was untruthful on one issue, they often disregard subsequent statements.

4. Jurors must be able to RECALL the testimony of your witnesses. After days, and sometimes weeks or months of testimony, jurors must be able to remember what a witness has said so that deliberations reflect what you want them to consider in their discussions. The most memorable testimony is that which is received as a series of "sound bites." These are short phrases or sentences that capture the essence of what the witness is trying to say, in a succinct way. Sound bites are more easily recalled than long, rambling narratives. Testimony must also get into their notes accurately if it is to carry weight. If jurors are not

allowed to take notes, it is doubly important that testimony be memorable. There are ways to enhance each of these requirements when a witness is properly prepared.

5. Jurors must LIKE your witness, or at least have a positive feeling toward him or her. Social research has shown that people tend to believe those they like, and to disbelieve those they dislike. Jurors who perceive a witness to be personable, forthcoming, genuine, confident (but not arrogant), and friendly are more likely to also believe their testimony, particularly if it clashes with a witness they dislike, regardless of veracity.

Traditional Preparation Strategies Are Rarely Effective

Traditionally, attorneys pull their witnesses aside fifteen to thirty minutes before the deposition is to begin, or a few minutes before a witness is to take the stand, and share some words of wisdom or last-minute admonishments: "Listen carefully," "Don't talk too fast," "Stick to your story and don't let the other attorney bully you," or "Try not to be nervous." While helpful, this hallway advice has little staying power, and many attorneys have shaken their heads after an adverse outcome, wondering how the witness could have possibly testified so poorly when the facts appeared so straightforward.

A slight improvement on this strategy is to meet with a witness several hours or days before the scheduled appearance to instill a more thorough set of "rules" that should govern their testimony. Long, often confusing laundry lists of do's and don'ts are reviewed while the witness's eyes glaze over in wonder and concern about how to possibly remember all the rules when under the pressure of cross-examination in a room full of strangers. Even worse, what are the consequences of failing to follow one or more of the attorney's directives? When it comes to effective witness preparation, a limited, uniform routine is simply not effective.

Effective Preparation Strategies

The most effective way of preparing witnesses involves a much more thorough, organized, and comprehensive process during which the witness's communication patterns and needs are carefully assessed and an individualized preparation approach is crafted. The witness is educated and advised, given opportunities to practice various types of questions, provided with feedback and suggestions about improving effectiveness, and offered opportunities to have questions answered and anxieties eased.

Sensitized to the needs of individual witnesses, having a plan that focuses on the witness's specific needs, and armed with specific skills to carry out the plan, attorneys can build a strong attorney-client relationship and enjoy a competitive advantage in the courtroom. It is an investment of time and commitment that pays big dividends when the witness provides compelling, convincing testimony that supports the case themes and facts. Using the methods and techniques described in this book benefits both the witness and the attorney immeasurably.

Jurors Expect Witnesses to Be Prepared

In conducting pre-trial research and post-trial interviews with jurors, we have learned an important fact: jurors expect witnesses to have been adequately prepared by their attorneys. One of the most frequent criticisms we hear is "Mr. Jones was not believable on the stand. I don't understand why his attorney did not prepare him better." People who serve on juries anticipate that by the time a case has come to trial, the attorneys are playing their "A" game and have not only prepared their evidence and exhibits carefully, but have also adequately prepared the witnesses who will provide testimony. A witness who performs poorly on the stand is believed to be reflective of the weakness of the case in general, or the inadequacies of the attorney.

On the other hand, an overly-prepared witness can generate a negative response from jurors. Witnesses who appear scripted, coached, or who have memorized answers will not be believed. The balance between adequately preparing and over-preparing a witness is a delicate one.

Attorneys Also Benefit from Witness Preparation

There are many benefits of witness preparation to the attorney. Most attorneys get considerable practice in law school about how to conduct cross-examination of witnesses, but they get much less experience with direct examination. Often, such experience is gained only at trial, and attorneys with little trial experience are at a distinct disadvantage. In the same way, most witnesses have little awareness of how they should respond under direct examination by their own attorney. Although witnesses are encouraged to display the same demeanor under cross-examination as they would under direct, this makes little sense if the witness is unfamiliar with the direct examination process. Witness preparation sessions provide that important opportunity.

In our experience, attorneys can sometimes discover new facts, additional details, or witness concerns that are revealed for the first time in a witness preparation session. Discovering that a defendant doctor possesses additional details regarding a patient chart entry, that an engineer plans to suggest an alternative theory of weight distribution not previously considered, or that an eyewitness now expresses doubt about her observations, will enable an attorney to avoid potential embarrassment in the courtroom.

Not Just Pre-Trial, but Pre-Deposition Preparation Is Essential

Many attorneys are willing to spend time preparing witnesses for trial, but they don't take the time to prepare them for a deposition. If you wait until after the deposition, the testimony is committed and you now have to live with it. As consultants, we have often been contacted post-deposition by an attorney who is lamenting the poor performance of his or her witness. The attorney had the mistaken belief that the witness would be effective because he or she was a "successful person who was accustomed to speaking with authority" or "has given testimony in the past" and thus needed no pre-deposition preparation. The lesson learned? Every witness, and every attorney, can benefit from pre-testimony preparation. Helping your witness before deposition means you won't regret his or her performance later.

CHAPTER 2

THE VIEW FROM THE WITNESS CHAIR

Witnesses coming to your office to prepare to give testimony in legal matters arrive with a wide range of emotions and attitudes: anger, fear, resentment, overconfidence, apprehension, naïveté, and shaky composure. Some will surprise you when questioned. The confident, self-possessed witness may fall apart; the timid, overwrought witness may come through like a trooper. Most will require some level of education, practice, guidance, and reassurance if they are to be a help to your case and not a liability.

Not All Witnesses Are Equal

Witnesses vary considerably in how familiar they are with the legal process, how insecure and fearful they are about legal challenges, how receptive they are to feedback, how capable and motivated they are to take your advice, how motivated they are to cooperate in their defense, and how willing they are to talk about personal, sensitive, and incriminating matters. The fact is that witnesses, because they are human, come in all emotional shapes and sizes. Guiding a witness through a strange and intimidating legal process is one of the greater challenges you will face as a trial attorney.

Most of what people know about the legal process they have

learned from John Grisham novels or from television shows like *Boston Legal*, *LA Law*, and *The Practice*. They think smart lawyers can "get them out" or "get them off" with aggressive dialogue. They believe an entire trial can be concluded in a few hours, and that witnesses can be maneuvered into confessions on the stand, much as Perry Mason often accomplished in a few minutes of clever cross-examination. In reality, witnesses are often surprised at how long it takes for a lawsuit to go from Complaint to Verdict—often years in civil cases—or how much time is needed for discovery.

Preparing witnesses well is extremely challenging because your clients are rarely legal eagles. You must teach them how the legal system works, and what you must teach them is generally new to them and contains language that sounds foreign and threatening. And you must do this in a few short hours. As litigation consultants who have assisted with several thousand witness preparation sessions, we understand the challenges you often face.

Through the Eyes of the Witness

We also see the challenge from the other side of the table. Most witnesses arrive at a preparation session reluctantly, with a host of anxieties about what they will be doing and why, and with a pervasive sense of dread because they are being summoned to an attorney's office. Some are angry and resentful about being involved in a lawsuit they believe is groundless or in which they feel they played no part. Others are overconfident or falsely confident, arrogantly assuming they can outsmart opposing counsel and expose the frailties of his or her case. Being sensitive to what they are thinking and experiencing establishes the level of rapport attorneys need in order to conduct productive sessions with witnesses.

Performance anxiety is one of the most common fears among the general public. Whether speaking at a Rotary Club meeting, delivering a eulogy, or answering questions at a deposition or trial, most people get very anxious when they are "in the spotlight." Preparing a witness without addressing this anxiety would be an incomplete and perhaps ineffective preparation. Although attorneys are not trained psychologists, a few practice tips in this chapter can be very useful in calming the anxious witness.

Stressors of Giving Testimony

It is a rare witness who does not experience a variety of stressors when faced with the need to give effective and convincing testimony to a judge, jury panel, or board of fact finders. These stressors include the following examples:

- An unfamiliar environment of courtrooms, attorney offices, and court reporting facilities
- Unfamiliar faces, such as bailiffs, attorneys, court stenographers, judges, and jurors whom they do not know but must speak to openly and honestly
- An unfamiliar process, including strange and different language and rules
- Unnatural communication situations that differ from normal daily interaction and communication
- Fear and loathing of attorneys and the legal system, often based on prior bad experiences or media-fueled stereotypes of aggressive attorneys or corrupt judges
- Unrealistically high self-expectations to know all the right answers and be able to persuade others or risk damaging their case
- Fear of forgetting or having a poor memory for critical events
- Dread of lawyer questioning traps or having one's credibility questioned
- Fear of hurting the case or assuming the burden of winning it

- Strong negative emotions about being involved in a frightening and intimidating process

Nearly every witness carries some or all of these stressors. Being aware of this, and letting a witness know you are sensitive to his or her worries and concerns, helps build rapport. It also reminds you that while you reside in the legal world of motions, judgments, verdicts, testimony, and evidence, most people do not. To them, the legal arena is frightening and filled with potential dangers. Even attorneys who find themselves in the uncomfortable position of testifying in a legal matter can relate to some of these concerns.

The Intimidation Factor

Law offices and courtrooms are not only intimidating and anxiety-provoking, they are also antagonistic. Witnesses are often frightened of difficult questions being asked by highly educated, intelligent people who know the law. They fear they may freeze or panic on the witness stand. They fear an aggressive attorney may manipulate their words or extract untrue admissions. They fear being forced to reveal embarrassing, private, or incriminating information. They fear they will be "bad" witnesses who jeopardize the case, perhaps even causing the attorney to lose it. These fears accompany them to preparation sessions, and they cannot always be dispelled.

Oftentimes, merely explaining to witnesses what will occur at the deposition or trial can induce anxiety. Telling a witness that a written record will be made of everything that is said in the deposition, and that segments of the deposition could be referenced at trial, sounds frighteningly similar to the Miranda instruction: "Everything you say can and will be used against you." Knowing that one's words are being locked in forever by a court stenographer or officially recorded on video is enough to give anyone sweaty palms. Added to this early warning is the use of alien language such as "discovery," "objections," and "cross examination." To a witness, it can all sound very intimidating and anxiety-provoking.

Helping to Manage Fear and Anxiety

What can be done to help witnesses manage their worries and fears? It is not enough to simply instruct them to relax, and it is the rare witness who can do so completely. The following are some helpful techniques for combating common witness fears and feelings of intimidation:

- Remind witnesses that they are not responsible for the outcome of the legal proceedings. The witness may play a significant role, but other testimony, evidence, and facts are also important. Short of an admission of guilt, no single response at deposition or trial is going to "sink the ship" and lose the case.
- Remind them that while attorneys and judges are experts in the law, witnesses are also "experts" who possess their own experience, knowledge, and skill—whether it is in parenting, auto mechanics, medicine, business management, homeownership, banking, or any other area of work and life. They are not expected to know the law—that is the attorney's role—but to be experts in what they are testifying to. In that regard, they share the same status as attorneys or judges.
- Recognize that their anxiety is authentic. It is normal in legal situations. Suggesting they "not worry" can only set up unrealistic expectations that will compound anxiety. Give them permission to feel some anxiety as a normal reaction to an unusual situation.
- Educate them as much as possible about the essentials of the legal process in which they are involved, and provide ample preparation time. Knowledge and understanding are the most effective tools for combating anxiety.

- Provide practice in listening to and responding to questions so they gain confidence in their ability to handle whatever inquiry is set before them. Confidence and preparation combat intimidation.

What Makes Witnesses Ineffective

People aren't born bad witnesses. They are ordinary people with a range of communication skills, motives, and personality features that contribute to or detract from their performance as witnesses. As witnesses, many people are poor listeners because they are accustomed to "conversation," not question-and-answer formats. This means they often do the following:

- Engage in "out listening"—listening only long enough to get the "gist" and then their attention wanders until something else captures it
- Engage in "selective listening"—hearing only what they want to hear, filtering out all else
- Engage in "challenge listening"—formulating arguments to refute or challenge before they hear the entire question
- Attempt to mentally improve what is being asked because it is unclear to them
- Tolerate "little white lies," embellishments, boasting, and exaggerations because they themselves often engage in these conversation fillers
- Allow anxiety to interfere with processing or responding to the words being said (also known as "choking" or "freezing")
- Make false assumptions about how well others have understood them
- Try to "out think" the questioner in an attempt to direct the questioning or anticipate what will be asked next

In addition to these listening errors, witness effectiveness can also be jeopardized by the following factors:

- An innate motivation to explain, to be clear, and to be understood
- A strong desire to tell their story as quickly and candidly as possible
- A compulsive need to be thorough and complete, including minor details
- A helpful personality, reflected in the need to help, support, and facilitate opposing counsel's efforts to obtain information
- A need or desire to "please" the questioner and appear compliant
- Strong emotions (anger, fear, resentment) that can interfere with clear thinking
- Lack of confidence or feelings of intimidation fostered by media portrayals of attorneys "tearing down" a witness
- Defensiveness and the powerful motivation to defend and protect oneself

Perhaps the most common barrier to witness effectiveness, however, is lack of preparation. The remainder of this book addresses the when and how of overcoming barriers to effective witness communication and preparing witnesses to be more effective truth tellers. As with most strategic approaches, identifying and setting objectives is a good starting point.

CHAPTER 3

SETTING AND ACHIEVING OBJECTIVES FOR WITNESS PREPARATION

Witness preparation sessions have nothing to do with altering personalities or performing magical "make-overs." They are not designed to program or coach witnesses about what to say, provide opportunities for memorizing answers, or help witnesses re-construct events in a more favorable context. Even if such goals were possible, and they rarely are, they are largely illegal and unethical. However, establishing specific objectives for a witness preparation session enables the attorney to use time and resources wisely and ensure the session is effective *for that witness.*

Goals of Witness Preparation

The specific goals of witness preparation sessions are largely dictated by the role the witness is to play—how important is the testimony to the case, how much information does the witness possess, what is the level of involvement of the witness in the events at issue, and so on.

The witness whose testimony is limited may require little or no preparation at all. By contrast, a witness who is also a party and whose testimony is central to the case may require considerable preparation, as there will be many more needs and concerns.

Expert witnesses are a special category because they play very precise roles at trial. Their preparation is the subject of several excellent books (see Appendix C for these and other helpful resources), but many of the tips and techniques discussed in this book also apply to experts.

The overall objective of systematic and comprehensive witness preparation is simple and straightforward—to help a witness become an "effective truth-teller." This means focusing on the following issues:

- Explaining the process and answering questions
- Assessing and addressing the specific needs of the witness
- Clarifying roles and responsibilities
- Discussing mutual expectations
- Developing case and witness themes for organizing testimony
- Providing feedback and guidance
- Building witness confidence
- Improving the witness's sense of control over testimony
- Addressing body language and nervous habits
- Enhancing jury appeal and physical appearance

It is up to the attorney, based on the needs of the witness and other constraints such as available time and resources, to determine which goals are necessary and appropriate for a given preparation session. Let's examine the most common witness preparation objectives and why they are important.

Explaining the Process and Answering the Questions

Law office conference rooms, judges' chambers, and courtrooms are very familiar places to attorneys. Legal professionals also understand the roles of bailiffs, court stenographers, and judicial assistants. They know legal terms and rules of order in courtrooms. They know the law and its nuances. But it is a rare witness who has such familiarity. Witnesses can suffer sleeplessness, loss of appetite, stress-induced palpitations, and stomach upset at the mere thought of giving testimony under oath. Thus, witness preparation sessions can be equated to pre-birth "Lamaze" classes for expectant parents—it doesn't make the process painless, but it significantly reduces anxiety associated with the unknown. (See Chapter 6 for specifics on what a witness most likely needs to know when being prepared for a deposition, trial, or hearing.)

Some attorneys assume witnesses should be informed on a "need to know" basis. It is a serious mistake to make this assumption. While it is wise to refrain from dire predictions or lofty guarantees regarding trial outcomes, it is the rare witness who would prefer to know less than to know more. Invite your witnesses to express their frustrations, fears, and concerns so they may become more confident in your support and more committed to the preparation process. It is good practice to begin the session by inquiring what is worrying the person most, or what has been a source of stress in preparing for the session. Asking a witness, "What is troubling you most about this case or our meeting today?" will provide insight into the client's foremost concerns.

Assessing Strengths and Needs

When it comes to witness preparation, one size does not fit all. No two witnesses are the same, so cookie-cutter witness preparation is unlikely to be effective for every witness. This is where witness-centered preparation comes in.

Witness-centered or "witness focused" preparation means making the individual witness's needs and concerns, not the attorney's agenda, the focus of the preparation session. It requires listening to the witness carefully to understand his or her worries and anxieties, identifying areas in which the witness lacks confidence, and assessing the witness's communication strengths and challenges. Then the preparation session can be designed around the needs and goals for the witness, whether it is education and explanation, guided Q&A practice, correction of communication problems, bolstering of confidence, grooming advice, or a combination of those goals. The following chapter focuses on how to assess your witness's needs, strengths and weaknesses so you can tailor the preparation with specific objectives in mind.

Clarifying Roles and Responsibilities

Just like a character in a play, it is important for witnesses to understand their role in the legal process and the purposes of their testimony. Knowing what their testimony is intended to accomplish (e.g., provide key facts, establish motive, explain losses, describe the timeline of events, etc.) gives witnesses appropriate context for their testimony. Defendant doctors, for example, should not be confusing their role with that of a medical expert; family members should not confuse their roles with those of therapists or police investigators; and researchers should not confuse their roles with those of consumers. Clarifying a witness's role brings understanding about why the person will or will not be asked certain questions, or on the other hand, why the person should be prepared to respond to inquiries in specific areas. Witnesses who understand their role in the events at issue in a lawsuit are better able to put their answers into the context of that role. They have a core of understanding that serves as a frame of reference when answering specific questions.

Knowing the boundaries of their roles and responsibilities enables witnesses to "stay inside the box" that is directly related to their involvement and to refrain from answering questions that go beyond their experience, expertise, or knowledge. If relevant, encourage witnesses to clarify their responsibilities as they relate to the events at issue in the case. For example:

> *"It was my responsibility to provide the Board of Directors with regular financial reports, but it was the CEO who made decisions about allocation of resources."*
>
> *"Nurses are responsible for observation and reporting regarding patients, but it is not in our scope of practice to diagnose medical conditions."*
>
> *"You would have to ask the driver of the van what training he had. Although I hired him, I was not responsible for his training."*

Many witnesses are relieved to hear that they are not only allowed, but encouraged to limit their testimony to what they personally know, saw, did, or thought.

Setting Mutual Expectations

Your expectations for a witness will vary, depending on whether the witness is being prepared for deposition, a hearing, or trial. There are different expectations associated with being a testifying party, a fact witness, or an expert witness. Inform each witness what needs to be accomplished in his or her testimony, and what simply cannot be reasonably achieved.

When preparing a witness for a deposition, it is important to explain the purpose of depositions, how they are conducted, and how the question-answer format differs from normal conversation. It is critical for witnesses to understand that simply telling their side of the story in a deposition is very unlikely to persuade opposing counsel to dismiss the case for lack of merit.

When setting expectations for witnesses preparing to give testimony at trial, on the other hand, it is important for the witness to understand it is rarely possible for a jury to fully understand what an injured plaintiff or victim's family has been through. Witnesses must also understand the difference between deposition and trial testimony, and between direct and cross-examination. Those who lack this basic understanding could apply the wrong rules when giving testimony.

Be certain to explain to your witness that pre-deposition or pre-trial preparation is not only lawful, but also ethical and practical. If witnesses are asked what they have done to prepare for their deposition, encourage them to reply that they have met with their attorney and reviewed relevant records or reports. If they are asked if they were prepared by a professional witness coach or litigation consultant, you should instruct them not to answer that question, as this would invade attorney-client privilege. If you expect your witness to be pressed on this issue, suggest how inquiries such as this should be handled. The honest reply to such an inquiry is that the witness received guidance from a communication specialist who helped them become a better listener and to give candid and accurate answers. The witness should never agree that answers have been "scripted," "coached" or "prompted" by anyone. (See Chapter 11 for a more complete discussion of discoverability issues.)

Developing Case and Witness Themes

Every case has a "theme" or unifying story about what happened, why it happened, who was fault, and how the injury can be rectified. Witnesses also have a story about how and why they were involved, what information they possess, and why their testimony is important. Before giving testimony, every witness should know his or her theme, even if it is as simple as "I observed the way in which Driver X was maneuvering recklessly through traffic." Attorneys often fail to involve the witness in developing or clarifying the case theme(s), and this can be a mistake. When witnesses are invited to contribute their thoughts and opinions about the central issues in the case, they have greater clarity about how their testimony fits into the case theme and the attorney's overall strategy.

What is meant by a case storyline or theme? In his helpful guidebook on opening statements and closing arguments, trial consultant Ronald Matlon (see Appendix C for reference) argues the importance of unifying case themes, and suggests a process for developing them. There may be more than one unifying theme in a given case, but the number should be limited. Dr. Matlon suggests several universal themes such as the "underdog," "the victim," and "the undefeated." However, the theme or themes of a case must grow from the facts and circumstances of the specific case and should not be superimposed. Below are some examples of case-specific and witness themes.

Sample Case or Witness Themes

- *"This case is about personal responsibility and misplaced blame."*
- *"Safety isn't something you concern yourself with only when an obviously dangerous situation arises. It has to be a concern every day when you are working on a construction site."*
- *"There was a less than satisfactory outcome for Ms. Smith, despite the careful surgery, which was complex and challenging."*
- *"The crane is a safe piece of equipment when it is operated in a safe manner, and it was not."*
- *"I understand that many people have lost trust in big corporations, but corrupt behavior would not be tolerated in Company X. For us, people come before profits."*
- *"The philosophy of that police officer was to shoot first and ask questions later. Well, there will be no later for Jimmy. He was shot twice and died at the scene."*
- *"The rules of the road aren't just for some people. They are for all drivers. When they get behind the wheel of an automobile, every driver has a responsibility to obey those rules."*

- *"Company Z was concerned with cutting corners and making money, and what it cost them was the safety of their customers."*
- *"I was doing my job and my performance evaluations show this. My firing had nothing to do with performance and everything to do with prejudice."*
- *"Con artists are like chameleons—they blend in and hide in the bushes. You don't see them until your money is gone, and so are they."*

A witness who is knowledgeable about the overall theme of the case, and of the purpose (theme) of his or her testimony, can reflect that theme in the testimony. This is important because it is the repetition of a case's theme or story throughout the trial, from opening statement to closing argument, that sets the framework for how jurors view the case.

Providing Feedback and Guidance

Most attorneys would agree their primary goal is to win the case for their clients. But an attorney's primary *advocacy* goal is to ensure witnesses are well-prepared and advised—to provide guidance and suggestions about how to listen to questions and how to handle difficult ones. This helps reduce a witness's anxiety about how questions are likely to be asked, how to recognize potential "traps," and how to be the best possible communicator under difficult circumstances. It is also up to the attorney and the communications consultant (if one is used) to provide feedback to witnesses about the effectiveness of their responses and how they are likely to be viewed by jurors and others. The feedback process builds confidence and enhances credibility. Question-answer (Q&A) practice improves basic communication skills such as careful listening and thoughtful responding. Providing guidance on demeanor, dress, and attitude helps a witness make a good impression.

Providing practice and feedback is more than merely telling a witness what *not* to do. You must also provide guidance about what will be most effective, accurate, or understandable. Remember that it is not only *what* the witness will say, but *how* he or she will say it. The goal is not only to tell the truth, but to do so effectively. Although it is tempting to simply tell a witness what you consider the most effective answer to a potential question, this approach rarely produces the intended effect. This is because the words used by an attorney or communications consultant are not the witness's own words. It is critical that witnesses answer questions in their own words, even if the answers appear less articulate than you would prefer.

Some witnesses accept and incorporate feedback easier than others. People who are high self-monitors are typically more receptive to feedback because they are more sensitive to how others see them and have greater needs to be socially accepted. Low self-monitors, on the other hand, are more oblivious to how others see them, have less sensitivity to reactions from others, and do not incorporate feedback and guidance easily. This is especially true for those who may have narcissistic personality traits or those who are not accustomed to receiving constructive feedback. With the latter witnesses, you may have to couch feedback in a less threatening or direct way, such as "You will be better understood if you..." (See Chapter 9 for additional suggestions on preparing witnesses who pose special challenges.)

Building Witness Confidence

Psychologists largely agree that some level of stress or anxiety actually enhances performance. But when fear and anxiety interfere with a witness's ability to think clearly, respond accurately, or control nervous gestures, it is no longer a helpful factor. In fact, if emotional roadblocks are not adequately addressed, the preparation session is not likely to be productive, and there will be little carry-over.

Here are some examples of what witnesses have said about their testimony when they were not properly prepared and lacked confidence in their answers:

From the Mouths of Unprepared Witnesses

- *"I was nervous about the aggressiveness of the other party's attorney. I didn't expect that."*
- *"I have painful memories about not being able to say what I wanted to say."*
- *"I kept trying to give good answers to bad questions."*
- *"It was much worse than I expected. I wasn't prepared for some of the questions [he] asked and I got confused."*
- *"I was so nervous I forgot everything. I probably looked like an idiot."*
- *"I just said 'I don't know' a lot. That's what I thought I was supposed to do."*
- *"I was asked questions in areas I didn't think were relevant to the lawsuit. I was surprised [opposing counsel] could do that, but I learned that at a deposition, apparently everything is fair game."*
- *"I couldn't sleep the night before the deposition. And I never have trouble sleeping!"*
- *"I just didn't want to be manipulated, but I found out [attorneys] have ways of asking questions to get you to say what they want to hear."*
- *"I was so afraid [the attorney] would get me to say something wrong."*
- *"When I finally read my deposition, I realized I had talked way too much and said some things that made me look bad. But it was too late."*

The time to help witnesses manage their expectations, stresses and concerns is before, not after they give their testimony. Helping witnesses to manage anxiety is challenging, but absolutely essential to preserving their likeability and credibility. Assistance from a professional may be necessary. When it is not feasible, try these techniques:

- Practice cognitive rehearsal, including positive self-talk.
- Introduce relaxation techniques, such as slow-paced breathing.
- Progress the questioning from least anxiety-provoking to most anxiety-provoking, allowing the witness to adapt to increasing levels of anxiety.
- Imagine positive outcomes such as, "Imagine jurors nodding in agreement as you speak," or "Picture your attorney smiling at you as you leave the stand."
- Visualize opposing counsel asking questions in an absurd or laughable scenario (e.g., in his or her pajamas or using a monkey puppet).
- Have the witness visualize answering questions as he or she wants to see themselves, responding with confidence and self-assurance, or as a mentor or respected colleague might answer questions.

It is also a good idea to give your witness permission to be a little nervous. Who wouldn't be? Admit that even you would be, in these circumstances. Perhaps describe your own nervousness at having to give testimony in some past context. While most of us resist feelings of nervousness or anxiety, in reality they are part of life. The key is to limit those feelings so they do not interfere with effective listening and speaking. A modest amount of anxiety can actually facilitate performance; high anxiety can block it.

Improving Control over Testimony

One of the defects of the question-answer method by which testimony is elicited from a witness is that the question often dictates the answer. Often so much so that what is relevant from the witness's point of view is left out. Most people remember events as complete stories rather than isolated facts, and they may feel frustrated when unable to tell the complete story.

For example, in preparing for a deposition, some witnesses erroneously conclude that if they simply "tell the story" of what happened, the opposing attorney will realize he or she doesn't have a case and they will dismiss the lawsuit, or they will realize the plaintiff has a very strong case and they will offer to make a large monetary settlement. This is another myth the attorney must address in the preparation session. The deposition is definitely NOT the place to tell one's complete story. It is simply to answer appropriate questions honestly and succinctly. This is why practice with the Q&A format is so important. It teaches witnesses the process of dealing with isolated, often non-sequential questions about events at issue.

Witnesses also often believe that because a highly educated, intelligent professional is asking questions, every question must be a good one, and every question deserves a correct and complete answer. Address this assumption in the preparation session. Witnesses must learn that the only questions they are required to answer are those that are completely understood. It is not unusual, for example, for a witness to get a poorly-worded question and then take responsibility for mentally improving it and answering that improved version.

The pressure to give an intelligent and complete answer can also prompt some witnesses to give any answer, even if the question calls for expertise or knowledge they do not personally possess, such as in the following cases:

Examples of Inappropriate Speculation

- *"I'm not sure what you're asking, but I think [action] is what we did when we heard the company was going bankrupt."*
- *"I don't recall what happened, but I assume that [action] occurred shortly after the bang."*
- *"That's not my area, but I think radiology techs are responsible to document whether the patient was experiencing pain on the X-ray table."*
- *"I wasn't looking at the speedometer, but I would guess my speed at about fifty miles an hour."*

In an effort to be helpful and to appear informed and intelligent, many witnesses will speculate, make assumptions, or simply guess. Pre-testimony preparation can better prepare witnesses to recognize questions they should not be answering. Some attorneys describe this as teaching a witness to "stay inside his/her box" and not offer opinions or guesses. Helping witnesses to understand they should answer questions only about what they personally know for a fact; observed with their own eyes; or performed, thought, or concluded, is a key role for any attorney.

Addressing Body Language and Nervous Habits

Everyone has some nervous habit or gesture that "gives us away" regarding underlying anxiety or fear. Whether it is hair twirling, knuckle cracking, chair rocking, leg bouncing, or cuticle chewing, other people read these gestures as measures of our truth-telling. Many people pride themselves on being able to read body language such as crossed arms, avoidance of eye contact, hand wringing, looking at the ceiling, and other signs of nervousness. Often they are incorrect in their assumptions, but people often interpret certain gestures and movements as indicators about whether the witness is lying or telling the truth, exaggerating, conjuring up an advantageous answer, or avoiding a difficult question.

Identifying nervous habits or movements is an important step in diminishing them. How many times have you heard the confession, "Until you pointed it out, I had no idea I always do that when I'm nervous!"? Making a person aware of an annoying or distracting nervous habit can sometimes help the person control or eliminate it. But this is not always the case. If the nervous habit is not amenable to correction, let it be. Remember that you can't always change habits and actions that are ingrained. At best you may be able to deflate their impact when the witness is on the stand, as the following example from an actual witness statement demonstrates.

Q: Mr. Smith, have you ever testified before in a court of law?

A: No, this is my first time and I'm pretty nervous. When I get nervous, my hands start to sweat a lot and I notice that I rub them on my knees. So I must be pretty nervous today. I've never testified in court before.

Body language is also important if a deposition is being videotaped. While written transcripts do not reflect nervous ticks and long pauses, such communication patterns become all too obvious on film. Make certain you bring attention to gestures such as:

- Touching the face while speaking
- Covering the mouth or stroking beard or mustache repeatedly
- Playing with eyeglasses, pieces of hair, or clothing
- Swiveling or rocking in the chair
- Leaning back or crossing arms
- Wandering gaze or rolling the eyes

These body language cues are often read by others as evidence of nervousness, untruthfulness or deception. Making the witness aware of such gestures, and the need to attempt to control them, may be all that is needed. An effective witness sits tall in the chair, leans forward slightly, keeps the hands still, makes good eye contact, and keeps the feet flat on the floor to avoid rocking.

Enhancing Jury Appeal and Physical Appearance

It is not uncommon, but certainly uncomfortable, to be surprised by a witness's appearance when he or she arrives for a deposition or on the first day of court. While some witnesses, especially plaintiffs, believe it will enhance judge and juror sympathy to appear financially strapped, incapacitated, or downtrodden, a sloppy or careless physical appearance at a deposition or trial has the opposite effect. Arriving at court in a T-shirt and dirty blue jeans, with poorly groomed hair and multiple face piercings will not impress anyone, nor will it make a witness appear more sympathetic.

At trial, clothes really do "make the man [person]." Each juror is assessing a witness's credibility, including the manner of speaking, eye contact, pattern of speech, body language, and physical appearance. They are judging how seriously each party is taking the court proceedings and the respect or disrespect they have for the judicial system.

Ask your client what he or she is planning to wear, and advise the witness to make certain that clothing is clean and well-pressed. You may even ask the witness to wear to the preparation session what is planned for the deposition or court appearance so you can assess its appropriateness. Don't hesitate to suggest a haircut. Female witnesses should be told to tie back long hair away from the face and to wear minimal jewelry. All witnesses should dress conservatively, even if it means buying a new outfit or making a trip to the local second-hand store. Nothing about the witness's appearance should say, "Look at me!" When giving testimony, the jurors' focus should be on what the witness has to say, not on how flashy, inappropriate, untidy, or "hip" the witness's appearance is.

Some witnesses will suffer from a negative stereotype or generalized poor image associated with their class or cultural group. Corporate executives may need to be humanized; gang members may need to be individualized; extremists may need to be softened; wealthy parties may need to appear less affluent; religious zealots may need to appear less radical. The point is that while we are not suggesting witnesses be reconstructed to some conservative or normative standards, the more easily ordinary people can relate to them, the more effective they will be as witnesses. Remind such witnesses that you are not suggesting they change their personalities or their lifestyles, only that they recognize the importance of the impression they must make on ordinary people, the jurors.

Video Recording Question-Answer Segments

Video recording some practice Q&A sequences and playing them back can help a witness become more aware of distracting gestures so they can be replaced with more effective body language. Video recording can also be used effectively to allow the witness to "try out" or experiment with more effective ways of answering difficult questions. In this way, the witness has an opportunity to self-evaluate which approach is more effective—natural tendencies versus a more thoughtful and confident approach. Which manner of answering is likely to be more effective with jurors? Which demeanor more accurately reflects what the witness intends?

Be certain if you are videotaping Q&A segments that you make a statement at the beginning of the recording protecting the video as attorney-client work product. Otherwise, the video could be subpoenaed by opposing counsel.

CHAPTER 4

Witness Assessment

What a witness says on the stand is obviously important, but *how* the person gives testimony is equally, if not more important. Although many attorneys give lip service to this notion, few truly understand its implications. Both research and experience has borne out consistently that the witnesses who are most influential at trial do not necessarily hold the highest credentials or have the most information. Rather, they are often those who can testify in a clear, simple, and direct manner that is believable *not* to attorneys or judges, but to the ordinary citizens who will be deciding the case.

Not Just "What" Is Said, But "How" It Is Said

When preparing any witness, experienced attorneys know it is just as important to work on a witness's demeanor, body language, and communication style as on the content of the testimony. They know that jurors often rely more on their impression of the witness's credibility and believability than they do on the specific content of the testimony (which may or may not be recalled in detail during deliberations). A witness whose demeanor is composed, confident, and straightforward is perceived by jurors as an honest, likable person. On the other hand, a witness who displays anger, impatience, defensiveness, or nervousness on the stand is often disliked and perceived by jurors to be dishonest. What jurors see on the stand is what they assume represents the underlying personality of the witness, and judgments are often based on those assumptions. Some jurors make such judgments early in a trial, based on observations of parties and witnesses even before the testimony begins.

Distinguishing Between "Good" and "Bad" Witnesses

Every attorney can attest to having good and bad witnesses involved in their cases. But what makes a good or bad witness? If one were to poll attorneys across the country, there is likely to be agreement that the following factors characterize witnesses in each camp.

Effective Witnesses	Ineffective Witnesses
Appear honest and believable (do not exaggerate, misrepresent, or make inconsistent statements; make good eye contact)	Lack sincerity (act flippant, make inappropriate gestures, appear irreverent or campy, avoid eye contact)
Have credibility (possess relevant knowledge, willing to answer questions, appear forthright)	Dodge difficult questions (avoid, pander, stall, divert)
Are likeable (genuine, physically attractive, personable, demonstrate personal warmth)	Seem unlikeable (hateful, frightening, very unattractive, stand-offish, arrogant, threatening)
Have a respectable appearance (good grooming, conservative dress and hair, absence of unusual mannerisms)	Have a poor physical appearance (bad personal hygiene, outlandish dress or hair, militant tattoos)
Display a good attitude (attentive, respectful, cooperative, calm)	Show a bad attitude (cynical, sarcastic, hostile, judgmental)
Are careful listeners (wait for the question, ask for clarification, stay on point)	Are poor listeners (interrupt questioner, answer what they want to rather than what is asked, frequently claim to misunderstand)

Are effective truth-tellers (answer succinctly, qualify answers, speak with good volume and confidence, give consistent testimony, tell the truth)	Are ineffective truth-tellers (give inconsistent answers, misrepresent, exaggerate, lack confidence, mumble, use poor grammar)

Not all attorneys are fortunate enough to have "good" witnesses who will be telling their story in deposition or on the stand. The challenge is to help ineffective witnesses become better witnesses, and reinforce the effective behaviors of good witnesses.

The Five "Cs" of Effective Witnesses

Good witnesses reflect what we refer to as the Five Cs:

- **Confidence:** As reflected in demeanor, voice volume, posture, good eye contact
- **Competence:** As reflected in dress, demeanor, ability to articulate, intelligence
- **Conscientiousness:** As reflected in attention to detail and thoroughness
- **Compassion:** As reflected in expressions of empathy and genuine concern
- **Charisma:** As reflected in the ability to relate to others in a friendly and genuine way

Few witnesses reflect all five of the "Cs," but it is important to understand that witnesses are evaluated by jurors and judges on these critical dimensions. Part of each witness's preparation must include some attention to these five aspects of presentation. If a witness is lacking in one area, support and encourage demeanor and responses that reflect other strengths. For example, the scientist witness who lacks charisma can show strength in the areas of competence and conscientiousness; the realtor witness who appears to be rather haphazard with paperwork can balance this with a charismatic personality that endears him to jurors and with expressions of sympathy for the bad luck experienced by the homebuyer; the radiologist who lacks the patient relationship that would promote empathy can build credibility by demonstrating conscientious attention to detail and unshakable confidence in reading the imaging studies.

How can an attorney accomplish challenging goals for a less-than-stellar witness in a reasonable amount of time? What is productive in preparing witnesses and what is a waste of time? Answers to these questions rest with the ability to assess your witness's strengths, so they can be fortified, and on your witness's weaknesses or challenges, so they can be improved upon.

Assessing Strengths and Weaknesses

Not all witnesses demand the same level or type of preparation. People vary considerably in their ability to make a positive impression, listen carefully, express themselves accurately, and speak with conviction and confidence. It is a mistake to assume that every witness requires the same standard session, or the same level of assistance. Witness-centered preparation means tailoring education and guidance to the person's individual needs and concerns.

The first step in a thorough witness-centered preparation is to assess the witness on a variety of applicable dimensions. What should this include? At the end of this chapter is a sample assessment form that covers various areas of potential focus. As an attorney, you may want to add others. Your witness may also identify additional areas s/he wants to work on. The important point is that some yardstick is needed in order to determine the appropriate emphasis for a given witness. Remember that you can't improve or fix everything in a single preparation session, or perhaps even in several sessions. But a good starting place is to pinpoint those areas most in need of improvement, or those areas in which improvement is possible. The witness checklist can be helpful in deciding where to focus your efforts.

Start by reviewing each category of characteristics described on the left of the checklist, either before the witness arrives or with the witness at the beginning of the assessment. Then make notes in the right column about what specifically you intend to focus on. Remember that it is nearly impossible to improve everything you would like to work on (although we have seen some impressive transformations). Be realistic in focusing on those characteristics most critical to your witness's effectiveness.

Ways to Use the Witness Assessment Checklist

- Based on past meetings with the client, conduct the assessment prior to your preparation session so you arrive at the meeting ready to focus your efforts.
- Ask your witness to complete the checklist as a form of self-assessment, thus enabling the witness to identify his or her own strengths and weaknesses.
- If using a litigation or communications consultant, have the consultant complete the checklist during the preparation and compare notes about midway into the session to ensure you are in agreement on the issues of mutual concern.
- Complete the checklist both before and after the preparation session to determine progress made and decide if another preparation session is needed.

Regardless of how you decide to use the assessment checklist, and whether you use a formal or informal assessment process, an assessment step is essential. Then prioritize what you will focus on in light of your objectives, as well as your time and resource limitations. Given that you rarely have all the resources you would prefer to have, and that you do not always have responsive witnesses to work with, managing your expectations is an important part of the witness assessment process.

Witness Assessment Checklist

Model Witness Characteristics	Need to Work On
Legal experience: familiarity with the deposition or trial process, previously deposed or testified, has read books on giving deposition or trial testimony, has spoken with others who have experience with giving deposition or trial testimony, has some past experience with attorneys and judges, not overly intimidated by the legal process	
Personal appearance: appropriate dress, good grooming, professional appearance, absence of nervous gestures or facial grimaces, no distracting accent or speech impediment, does not appear immature or senile/befuddled for age	
Demeanor and confidence: good posture, good voice volume, emotionally composed, good eye contact and attention, confident handshake, self-assured but not arrogant	
Attitude and preparation: positive and cooperative, no overt animosity toward opposing party, no overt animosity toward other parties, no defensiveness or hostility, familiar with records or documents involved, has reviewed information as instructed by attorney	
Level of stress and emotional control: minimal anxiety, no distracting nervous gestures, remains cool under fire, controls negative emotion, not obsessing or ruminating about issues in the case, avoids talking too much as a mask for anxiety, not a "loose cannon"	

Model Witness Characteristics	Need to Work On
Listening skill: listens to entire question, pauses, avoids "out listening" and "challenge listening," avoids anticipating or improving questions, catches ambiguities or compound questions, catches inflammatory language and embedded assumptions, appears attentive to questioner	
Response patterns: asks for clarification, uses own words, avoids simple agreement, gives succinct responses (no rambling or tangents), gives detail when necessary, does not admit to errors or mistakes, offers no opinions outside area of expertise, challenges embedded assumptions, refuses to guess or speculate, avoids over-explaining, appropriate teaching and use of visuals (if preparing for trial)	
Competence: knowledgeable in area of specialty, current on certifications, adequate work experience, speaks as an authority in area of expertise, good ability to recall information and facts related to profession, articulate	
Compassion and juror appeal: appears sensitive and compassionate, uses opposing party's name, avoids "distancing" and professional jargon, personable, able to express sympathy without admitting fault	
No other issues or concerns: has reliable transportation, returns phone messages, is not getting contradictory advice from someone else, has no memory deficits due to brain injury, has no addiction issues, etc.	
Overall expected performance: Note your overall assessment of the witness's ability to provide honest and effective testimony	

CHAPTER 5

MANAGING YOUR EXPECTATIONS FOR WITNESSES

Most trial attorneys dream about the perfect witness: the expert who carries the trial with spellbinding and convincing medical testimony; the accident victim whose poignant description of injuries and losses brings tears to the eyes of the most stoic juror; the forthright employee who can provide specific and detailed examples of harassment experienced nearly every day on the job. But the reality is that most witnesses will be less than perfect, poor witnesses can be improved only slightly, and some witnesses may actually damage your case by becoming loose cannons on the stand. Adjusting your expectations to reflect the realities you will face with some witnesses is an important adaptive mechanism for any successful trial attorney.

No Such Thing as a Makeover

Witness-centered preparation is not a "makeover." Despite what the media or some attorneys believe, it is simply not possible to make witnesses into someone they are not. At best, you can educate, improve, and reassure. You cannot program or makeover a person—certainly not in a few hours. If that were possible, attorneys would have their own television reality show.

Train Wreck vs. Car Accident

Sometimes the best you can realistically accomplish with a witness is to keep him or her from being a complete disaster. Spokane (WA) attorney Brian Rekofke refers to this as "turning a train wreck into a mere auto accident" in terms of the severity of the repercussions. The substance and process of good communication is much too complex to assume it can be taught in a few hours to a reluctant witness. You may have to settle for an outcome that is survivable.

Face Reality

Realistically, not every person will be a good (i.e., credible, effective, influential) witness, no matter how much effort you devote to preparation. When your witness is a "train wreck," identify a few key areas in which you believe some improvement can be made, and focus on those, given your time and resource constraints.

It May Require More Time and Effort

If, after three or four hours of preparation, you see little or no improvement in your witness, you have a decision to make: Will additional preparation be necessary and helpful, or will additional preparation be a waste of time? This is an important judgment call. Sometimes a seemingly hopeless witness merely needs additional preparation and the benefit is well worth the effort. As consultants, we have assisted in as many as four three-hour preparations after which there was significant improvement that would not have been thought possible on the basis of only one or two initial sessions.

This is a situation for which video recording of the preparation session may be a very useful tool. If you are comfortable with the idea, send the video home with the witness, along with instructions on how to use it for self-critique. The instruction might be as follows:

"Play a question and the answer that you gave, and then pause the recording. Next, ask yourself what may have been a better, more succinct, or more effective answer. Then, rewind and re-play the question, pause, and give the improved answer. Continue in this way through the most difficult parts of your testimony."

This self-help technique is likely to be most effective with a witness who is motivated to modify his or her communication skills in order to be a better witness. An unmotivated or overly self-critical witness is less likely to ever look at the video recording, much less use it for self-improvement.

Ability to Incorporate Suggestions

People vary in their ability to acknowledge areas in which improvement may be warranted, incorporate feedback, and make the necessary behavioral or attitudinal changes. Psychologists refer to this ability as "self-monitoring," and it can range from very low to very high. Low self-monitors tend to use inner beliefs and values in deciding how to behave, while high self-monitors tend to censor their surroundings and change their behaviors to fit in. Low self-monitors "say it like they see it" and have more difficulty adapting to the requirements of varying social situations. High self-monitors, by contrast, are able to adapt and show variability in behavior in different contexts; they can discern what kind of behavior is required in different contexts and make changes. In simple terms, some would describe low self-monitors as "rigid," while high self-monitors would be considered "flexible."

In a witness preparation session, those with a limited capacity for self-monitoring are less likely to make substantive change in communication areas identified as problematic. For example, even with prolonged practice, a low self-monitor is unlikely to incorporate a suggestion to slow down and be more thoughtful in answering questions if his or her normal style is to "think off the top of one's head" and be long-winded. It is up to you (and the consultant, if one is being used) to determine if additional sessions are likely to result in modification of this style.

Not All Witnesses See the Need for Preparation

As consultants, we sometimes hear attorneys complain that a witness is not willing to participate in a preparation session. The witness does not see the need, is too busy with other obligations, or simply wants to distance him or herself from the litigation process as much as possible. Sometimes the resistance is subtle: the witness will commit to only an hour or two, misses the appointment, or makes it difficult for the scheduler to find a time that works with his or her schedule. One solution to such roadblocks is persistence. Other suggestions for overcoming pre-deposition or pre-trial preparation resistance include the following ideas:

- Remind the witness that the session is for his or her benefit because the effectiveness of the testimony is directly related to the strength of the case.
- Employ the "readiness" theme: *"Opposing counsel and their team have spent months or years preparing this case. They have reviewed documents and planned carefully what they want to ask you. They are ready; you are not."*
- Use your powers of persuasion to argue that "preparation levels the playing field" because attorneys are experts at questioning witnesses but most people are not experts at being a witness. You do not want the person to be at such a disadvantage.
- Explain that witness preparation is a critical part of your role as an attorney—to ensure every advantage for the client.
- Send a formal letter from your office, including the enclosure contained in Appendix A, requesting participation in a preparation session as part of the trial preparation process. Be firm and straightforward.

- Indicate that the insurer (if appropriate) has authorized and endorses a preparation session.

People who have given testimony previously can be reluctant to attend a preparation session because they have "been there, done that" and feel they don't need any additional preparation. The following list provides some effective retorts.

Comebacks for the "I Don't Need It" Witness

- *"This is different. Different case, different facts, different attorneys, different jurors. You need to be prepared for your testimony in this specific case."*
- *"This will be a good opportunity for us to review what was effective in your past appearances and make improvements in testimony for this case."*
- *"I wouldn't be doing my job if we didn't have some time to make certain you are completely refreshed on the process and rules you will need in order to be well prepared in this case."*
- *"It will benefit both of us to review the areas of your testimony and the kinds of questions you are likely to be asked in this case. There is no downside to doing just that."*

Adequate preparation of witnesses is part of the "standard of care" for trial attorneys. That standard requires more than a few words of encouragement before entering the deposition meeting room or the courtroom. You are not properly representing your client if you allow a witness to answer questions from opposing counsel without thorough, adequate preparation. Failure to use all possible means to persuade a witness that s/he will benefit from pre-deposition or pre-trial preparation is to fall below that standard. Don't give up easily.

CHAPTER 6

What Your Witness Needs to Know

A competent coach would never consider taking a new team onto a playing field without first explaining the rules of the game, educating players about basic strategy, assessing each player's capabilities and limitations, and providing sufficient practice. The same is true of a competent attorney taking an inexperienced witness to a hearing, deposition, or trial. Witnesses who better understand how a case will be presented or defended by the attorney or trial team have a better grasp of their role and the expectations surrounding that role. Those who understand the various steps in the legal process and the goals of each phase are less anxious about the unknowns and appear more confident.

A Word about "Legalese"

Taking a few minutes to explain the legal process and familiarize a witness with basic legal terminology consistently pays off in increased witness confidence and a more relaxed performance. But keep in mind that the language you use in educating your witness could be off-putting. You speak in the language of lawyers, often called "legalese." But most witnesses speak in ordinary terms. Avoid lapsing into legalese with witnesses. Your use of terms unfamiliar to them, or bombarding them with a new language, can add to the intimidation factor. Don't assume ordinary people know what is meant by a "complaint" or even a "deposition." You need not attempt to impress a witness with your grasp of the law and your fluency with its language; s/he already acknowledges your expertise and will expect you to explain in ordinary terms.

Not Just the Facts, Ma'am

While witnesses need some basic education about the legal process, and how to answer questions effectively, they also need to be prepared on what is going to happen, when, and why. Basic logistics and procedures should also be covered. Never assume a witness knows who will be there, that s/he will be sworn to tell the truth, and that a court stenographer will be taking down every word spoken. Attending to the basics helps make the strange more familiar.

Deposition vs. Trial or Hearing

There are distinct differences between the role of a witness at deposition and the role of a witness at a hearing or trial. Depending upon the situation, explain the differences so your witness knows what is appropriate for that role. This is particularly important if your witness will first give a deposition, and then give testimony at a trial. Unless witnesses understand and appreciate the differences in roles, they can easily become confused and accuse you of giving them contradictory guidance.

The following table may be useful in explaining to your witness the important differences in roles:

Witnesses at a *Deposition*	Witnesses at *Trial*
Are subjected primarily to *cross-examination* by the opposing attorney	Are subjected to both *direct examination* by you and *cross-examination* by opposing counsel, as well as re-direct and re-cross
Are encouraged to answer *only* the question asked, in a succinct format	Need to answer questions *fully* under direct examination, providing context and explanations as appropriate
Must understand that this is *not* the place to "tell their story"	Must understand this is the place to *"tell their story"* to the jury, and the best time to do so is under direct examination by you
Should maintain *eye contact* primarily with the questioning *attorney*	Should be certain to make *eye contact with the jurors* as much as possible, especially on key answers or when giving long explanations
Should answer specific questions asked by opposing counsel, but *not* offer additional explanations	Must be an *"educator"* of jurors, rather than a plaintiff, defendant or expert witness
Understand *their attorney* is there primarily as an observer, to voice objections if necessary, and to ensure a proper record is made	Understand that their attorney is a *powerful advocate* who will present their side of the story and actively persuade the jury to decide in their favor
Are aware that *no judge or jury*—no decision-maker—is present	Realize a *jury* is present and these ordinary citizens will be deciding the case
Have been told that *objections* by their attorney will be noted for the record, but they will most likely have to answer all questions anyway, unless directed otherwise by their attorney	Must be told that objections by you will be *ruled on* by the judge before questioning can proceed
Realize the setting is rather *informal*, but the rules are formal	Can be intimidated by the *formal* and solemn setting

These differences make it important to prepare your witnesses for trial even though you may have amply prepared them for deposition. You will have given your witnesses certain guidelines for their deposition that no longer apply at trial, and it is critical that witnesses be aware that giving testimony at a trial is quite different, and that different rules apply. For example, imagine a female witness at trial who is still following the admonition to "be as brief as possible in your answers" when addressing a group of decision-makers who must trust and believe her if they are to decide the case in her favor. Her brevity could easily be interpreted as a failure to be forthcoming, or having "something to hide" from the jurors, and the negative consequences could be unintended.

Depositions: What Your Witness Needs to Know

Purposes of the Deposition

In preparing witnesses for deposition, it is important for them to understand that a deposition has several purposes, including the following:

- Gain information desired by the opposing party
- Validate opposing counsel's case "themes"
- Evaluate the witness's credibility and jury appeal
- Test the witness's emotional vulnerabilities and limits (by attempting to manipulate, intimidate, anger, frustrate, confuse, or confront the witness)
- Explore inconsistencies in testimony, or attempt to create them
- Commit the witness to a particular view of the facts that agrees with opposing counsel's own perception of what happened and why

Witnesses who understand the purposes of the deposition have a better framework for processing the information and guidance you will be providing, and for incorporating that guidance into the deposition's Q&A process.

The Logistics of a Deposition

If you are working with a witness unfamiliar with the process, explain the general procedures and rules that will be followed in the deposition, as this helps reduce unknowns and manage expectations. Some witnesses may be quite naïve and require the attorney to outline the most basic elements of the process. If a witness assessment has been completed, the attorney will already know how much or how little needs to be explained. However, it is best to avoid assuming the witness may know more than he or she actually does. Explain who will be in attendance, who has the right to be in attendance, who will be asking questions (and who will not), and about how long the deposition will likely last. Be certain to inform a naïve witness about the swearing in process, the roles of the court stenographer and videographer (if one is to be present), and the way in which objections will be handled. Make certain the witness knows the location, date, and time of the session.

The Essential Features

Depending on the relative experience or inexperience of your witness, some basic information about depositions and their mechanics may need to be explained. If necessary, you should cover the following essentials about the features of depositions.

A deposition is...	On the other hand, it is...
Giving testimony under oath before a trial begins; opposing counsel's opportunity to discover what you know before you testify at trial	NOT an opportunity for the witness to tell his or her story or attempt to convince opposing counsel that his or her client's case doesn't hold water
Only possible in civil cases, not in criminal cases (typically)	NOT the place to provide information that is beyond the scope of the question
Taken during the *discovery* phase of a lawsuit; conducted for some or all of the parties and key witnesses on both sides	NOT a normal conversation, but rather a series of specific questions that require specific, succinct answers
A question and answer format involving, at a minimum: the witness ("deponent"), the attorney asking the questions ("deposing attorney"), and the witness's attorney ("defending attorney")	NOT guided by the rules of social exchanges; it is NOT acceptable to embellish, hide a lack of memory, gossip, ramble, speak without thinking clearly, tell little white lies, or attempt artful sidesteps
An appropriate setting for being a good listener, alert, cautious, and thoughtful; "think before you speak" is a deposition mantra	NOT an appropriate setting to attempt to persuade, argue, blame, or become verbally combative
Video recorded and/or transcribed word-for-word by a court stenographer; a written transcript of the entire proceedings can be made available to all parties if requested; deponent has the right to review the transcript for errors (but only under certain circumstances can testimony be altered)	NOT an opportunity to attempt to out-wit opposing counsel, demonstrate opposing counsel's lack of knowledge, or to "educate" opposing counsel on any issue or event about which he or she appears confused or ill-informed
Typically two to four hours in length, but can last several days, depending on the complexity of testimony required of the witness	NOT an opportunity to assist opposing counsel to understand the technical aspects of the issues in the case, unless asked
Usually conducted in a law office conference room, but may occur in other settings	NOT an occasion to please, act sociably, charm, or attempt to ingratiate oneself with opposing counsel

How Objections Will Be Handled

Most people understand that attorneys may make objections to questions for various reasons, but their understanding of how objections are to be handled is mostly gleaned from television. They often do not know what is appropriate in a deposition setting. Be certain to explain the kinds of objections attorneys are allowed to make in a deposition, what different objections mean in lay terms, and what the witness should do if you make an objection. This is also a good time to reinforce the importance of pausing before speaking—it gives you an opportunity to voice the objection before the witness begins speaking. Explain that unless instructed by you to do otherwise, they will likely be asked to "answer if you can." Instruct your witness to ask for a re-statement of the question, as your objection may have interfered with a thought process.

Video-Recorded Depositions

It is an increasingly common practice today for opposing counsel to arrange to have the deposition video recorded. A number of motivations may underlie the decision to video record a witness's deposition. The reasons may include one or more of the following:

- Video captures behavioral cues that are not apparent in a simple typed transcript, such as defensive body posture, long pauses before answering, emotional expressions, and revealing voice intonation.
- The presence of a camera in front of a witness can add to the intimidation factor, thus heightening anxiety.
- Opposing counsel may wish to use portions of the video at trial, perhaps in the opening statement, to emphasize a particularly incriminating answer or to impeach the witness by demonstrating inconsistencies.
- Opposing counsel may be planning to conduct a pre-trial focus group or mock trial and wishes to assess mock jurors' reactions to the witness.

Regardless of the reasons, and they may remain unknown, the witness should be made aware of this possibility during the preparation session. Even if opposing counsel had not given notice that the deposition will be video recorded, the witness should be advised that it may still occur. Some attorneys are liberal in allowing video recording even if not indicated earlier, and it should not be a last-minute surprise to the witness.

If the deposition is to be video recorded, explain how this will make the situation a little different. The witness will need to be more cognizant of appearance, demeanor, facial expressions, and the use of pauses before answering. The most succinct advice is to instruct the witness that his or her demeanor should more closely approximate that which would be expected at trial. For example, while you may advise your witness to take a pause before answering a question, it will be important to limit the pause if testimony is being video recorded. Extensive pauses may be interpreted by viewers as a lack of confidence in the answer or an attempt to manufacture an answer that is more helpful to the deponent, but not completely truthful. The witness should also dress as s/he would for trial.

Surprisingly, witnesses whose depositions are video recorded often report they become so focused on listening and answering questions that they forget the camera is present, or they are able to ignore it. Share this with your witness to suggest they could easily do the same.

If you are fairly certain your witness's deposition will be video recorded, consider conducting the preparation session with a video camera in place. This will serve two functions: Q&A segments can be replayed during the preparation session for purposes of critique, and it will help desensitize the witness to the presence of recording equipment. Make certain you record a statement at the beginning of the recording, protecting the video as attorney-client work product.

Trial Testimony: What Your Witness Needs to Know

The Role of Educator, Not Witness

At a hearing or trial, the role of the witness is expanded beyond the mere answering of questions. In the courtroom, witnesses are in a position to be "juror educators" who are teaching the triers of fact what they know about the events or circumstances regarding their role in the case. For trial, prepare witnesses to *educate*, not to testify.

Thinking like a teacher instead of a testifier means the witness must do the following:

- Explain in terms that everyone can understand.
- Speak slowly so jurors can take notes (if allowed).
- Look directly at the jurors so they can judge the witness's credibility.
- Use examples with which jurors can identify (e.g., home, family, sports, etc.).
- Create visual images for jurors (e.g., "a hole the size of a walnut" or "pain that felt like a hot poker jammed into my back").
- Demonstrate with "props" such as drawings, models, mock-ups, charts, instruments, tools, or photos.
- Hold up a hand and tick off points on each finger.
- Apply the "Rule of 3"* and avoid making more than three specific points in an answer.

Teaching witnesses to *mentally preface* each of their answers with the phrase, "What jurors need to know about this is…" can also help

---

* The "Rule of 3" is a writing principle suggesting that things that come in threes (e.g., three little pigs, three stooges, Goldilocks and the three bears) are inherently more effective, and perhaps easier to remember, than any other number.

witnesses see their role in a less anxiety-provoking context. As a juror educator (or in some cases, an educator of a judge), witnesses are advised to avoid professional jargon and to speak in a language that ordinary people can understand. Tell witnesses, "Your goal is to become a good teacher of two rows of tenth graders. In other words, would a tenth grader understand your explanation?"

Watching the Language

It is important to remind witnesses that at trial, they are speaking to jurors, not to attorneys or judges. They must gear their language to ordinary people and make certain that if they use professional jargon, they explain what various terms mean. The use of professional jargon may be important to establish credibility, but it should then be explained in commonly used terms. A witness who "talks over the heads" of jurors will not be as effective as one who takes the role of "juror educator" seriously by ensuring that terms, jargon, and acronyms are explained in lay language.

This is especially true for expert witnesses who may assume their believability and juror impact reside in their voluminous resume and command of professional jargon. Nothing could be further from reality. Post-verdict interviews of jurors have indicated that the least effective expert witnesses were those who "tried too hard to impress us" and the most effective were those who connected with jurors on a genuine or personal level, used demonstrative aids, and used language they could easily understand.

The Steps of a Trial

If you are working with a witness who has never before been a witness at a trial, explain the general steps of a trial. You will be surprised how few people are aware of each step and their role, if any, at each step. Your explanation should include a brief description of what happens at each phase. A simple explanation is best and may include the following steps:

1. Arguments made in front of the judge before the jury is brought up
2. Introduction of the parties and their attorneys
3. A brief statement by the judge about the case and the parties involved
4. Jury selection and seating of the panel
5. Opening statements by each side, beginning with the plaintiff or prosecutor
6. Plaintiff's or prosecutor's claims and evidence are presented; witnesses are questioned by both sides
7. Defense's evidence and arguments are presented; witnesses are questioned by both sides
8. Closing arguments by each side, beginning with the plaintiff or prosecutor and followed by the defense
9. (Optional) Rebuttal argument by plaintiff or prosecutor
10. Jury instructions to the jury panel
11. Jury deliberations in which the panel discusses and decides specific questions (e.g., guilt, innocence, negligence, causation, allocation of fault, etc.)
12. Verdict delivered
13. (If appropriate) Sentencing

Some attorneys prepare a brief, one-page handout for witnesses containing these steps to ensure each phase is covered and that any questions they may have are answered. It is also helpful to explain to the witness where in this process their testimony will be required. If the witness is also the client who will be seated with you throughout the proceedings, describe the ways in which he or she can appropriately assist you during the trial. For example:

- Observing potential jurors during *voir dire* and noting any responses or behaviors that may be important to consider when deciding who to strike
- Alerting you if the client recognizes anyone in the jury venire
- Making notes about an expert's testimony that may require follow-up (if the client is also an expert in the field)
- Observing your questioning style so the client will be better prepared for your style of direct examination
- Observing the cross-examination style of opposing counsel to better prepare for questioning

Also helpful is a drawing that sketches the layout of the courtroom, indicating the placement of various court personnel, the witness box, the seating of the jury, etc. Most of this will be familiar to witnesses who watch television programs about trials. However, be aware that such programs may dispense inaccurate or incomplete information, and tend to focus on criminal trials, not civil cases.

Courtroom Demeanor

It is not unusual for jurors to look for extra-evidentiary clues about a witness's credibility and believability. They note body language and attempt to interpret its meaning. They scrutinize how parties in the lawsuit interact with their attorneys. They observe a party's general attitude about the proceedings. A witness who is also a party seated at counsel table is under scrutiny by jurors at all times, not just when s/he is on the witness stand. Counsel your witness to be vigilant about posture and attention, and to avoid inappropriate remarks or gestures when another witness is testifying.

This is especially true if you are seated very near the jury box. Jurors in post-trial interviews have been heard to remark about the thoughtless doodles of those seated at counsel table.

Consistency of Demeanor

It is tempting for witnesses to appear helpful and pleasant when being questioned by their own attorney, but become surly, argumentative, or uncooperative when being questioned by opposing counsel. After all, they are the enemy! But your witness must treat the opposing attorney with the same courtesy shown to you or a juror. A witness who remains respectful, patient, and calm during difficult questioning by opposing counsel gives jurors the impression that s/he has nothing to hide and no reason to become angry or defensive. While some jurors expect over-excited behavior on the part of attorneys, they are repelled by argumentative, defensive, and disrespectful behavior from a witness. Caution your witness to avoid the Dr. Jekyll-Mr. Hyde persona and demonstrate the same demeanor whether being cross-examined or being questioned by you.

CHAPTER 7

Steps in Conducting an Effective Preparation

When you prepare a witness is as important as *how* you prepare. Thorndike's Law of Recency holds that the most recent response is the one most likely to re-occur. The learning drop-off curve applies in witness preparation as it does in any form of instruction: the longer the time from the instruction, the more likely information will be forgotten.

Timing Is Important

The optimal time for witness preparation is shortly before the testimony is to be given—a few days at most. If a witness is to testify at trial, the closer the preparation is to the time the witness will take the stand, the better. As consultants we have assisted in the preparation of trial witnesses the night before they were to testify, and even on the morning they were to take the stand.

How long should a preparation session be? While excessive preparation is not only tiring but counter-productive, adequate time needs to be reserved for this important process. A good rule of thumb: two to three hours of preparation for every anticipated hour of testimony. This is particularly true if the witness has never before given testimony at a deposition or trial. However, the amount of time needed for adequate preparation of a witness depends on many factors—the role of the witness in the events at issue, the volume of records and documents the witness will be addressing, the prior litigation experience of the witness, the time and resources available to the attorney and witness, and many other variables. It is a judgment call on the part of the attorney. In our experience, we have rarely encountered an "over prepared" witness, but many who were under prepared.

Use Time Wisely

Being a witness in a lawsuit, whether a named party or a fact witness, is a disruptive and taxing imposition. People are busy, and the competing demands of work and family must often be further squeezed by making time for a preparation session. Without a concrete structure and purpose, preparation time can be wasted, little will be accomplished, and both you and your witness may be left with a feeling of frustration. In fact, a poorly conducted session can add to the confusion and anxiety a witness may already be experiencing.

Make the time you and your witness spend together as efficient and productive as possible. If you have assessed your witness thoughtfully, you should be able to focus on what your witness needs, and for what purposes. Outlining in advance what you expect to accomplish, and how the witness will benefit from the session will help to ease any concerns the witness has about how your time together will be spent.

Work around the witness's schedule and location if necessary. As consultants we have assisted attorneys in conducting sessions via international phone calls or teleconferencing, at kitchen tables, in empty hospital exam rooms and college classrooms, and at clubhouse assembly rooms. We have met with attorneys and their witnesses on weekends, evenings, and holidays. Be prepared to go where the witness can meet you, wherever and whenever that may be.

In the interest of saving time and effort, it may be tempting to "piggy-back" by preparing a witness for both a deposition and trial in one session. This will not yield the benefit you would hope. There are distinct differences in the preparation of a witness for deposition and preparing that witness later for trial. Mixing the two sets of rules will only confuse the witness and provide no gain.

The Preliminaries

Some people may see a preparation session as an opportunity for you, the attorney, to tell them what to say; others assume the session is necessary because you have already determined they are likely to be a poor witness for the case. Since neither is likely to be the case, you may want to send a brief letter to your witness (see Appendix A for a sample) before the session to set expectations about the process and outline the goals for the meeting. Most people are more motivated to attend a pre-deposition or pre-trial witness session if they know its purpose and how it will benefit them.

It is usually a good idea to begin a witness preparation session with an expression of empathy, using this opportunity to set a positive tone: "I'm sorry that you are involved in this legal matter; I know it can't be easy for you. Our session today should help to allay some of your concerns, and I expect it to be a productive meeting." Then explain what you will be doing with their time and what you hope to accomplish. (Appendix B has tips on the best way to begin a preparation session.) Assure witnesses that the preparation session is not being held because you think they will be ineffective, but rather to help them become more comfortable and confident.

It is also important to know if a witness is currently taking any medications or has any medical conditions that could affect his or her memory, stamina, or ability to concentrate or communicate. Certain medications can result in drowsiness, confusion, or the need to take frequent breaks. It is important for you to know if a witness is taking anti-depressants, anti-anxiety medications, or prescription opiates for pain, as these can affect cognitive processing and performance. A witness who is diabetic or who has a back problem may have special needs to be addressed not only in the preparation session, but in the deposition or the courtroom.

Listen First, Then Talk

The best initial step in any witness preparation session is to listen. Encourage the witness to express whatever has been on his or her mind in the past few days regarding the case. Give your witness an opportunity to share whatever is most concerning or upsetting, and to verbalize what issues he or she hopes will be addressed. You might begin, "I want to start by asking what is on your mind and what concerns and questions you have." Some concerns may trigger needed action on your part; others may simply require listening and compassionate responding. For example: "I understand all of this may be very upsetting for you. My hope is that this meeting today will help reduce some of that anxiety by increasing your sense of control over this process. Not knowing can be stressful."

Avoid answering questions with unnecessary "legalese," and be frank and upbeat. If reassurance is needed, focus on the positive aspects of the case or the weaknesses of the opposing party's case rather than on your years of experience or past trial successes.

Hear Their Story

One of the most productive ways to focus a preparation session is to ask witnesses to tell their stories in their own words. Here are some open-ended questions to get the witness talking.

Conversation Starters

- *How do you explain what happened? or What do you think happened?*
- *Why did it happen? or What do you think was the cause?*
- *Who did what wrong?*
- *Could anything have been done to alter the course of events or prevent the injury?*
- *Why are you suing the defendant?*
- *Why do you think you are being sued?*

Sometimes amazing things can be learned by taking a few minutes to listen to your witness—perhaps even information never before told to you. Listening to the witness's story also provides a baseline for assessing basic communication and speech patterns.

The beginning of a preparation session is an opportune time to find out what underlying emotions or tensions may be impacting your witness that have not yet been expressed. Is the witness also going through a difficult divorce, or having health problems? Is the witness worried about how to inform a spouse or close family member about the litigation? Is your witness concerned that actions at issue in the lawsuit could lead to the loss of his or her job, or impact his or her personal finances? Surfacing emotions and concerns in the preparation session is much preferred to seeing them unfold, unknown to you, at a deposition or on the stand.

Provide a Little Education

Some witnesses are seasoned veterans of the litigation process, but many have never been deposed or been inside of a courtroom. Depending on their prior experiences, the similarity of prior experiences to the current situation, or a witness's complete lack of experience with the legal system, some education may be needed. The amount of education needed will vary, depending upon the witness's prior experience, his or her role in the case, and the person's basic communication abilities. It will also depend upon whether the witness is being prepared for deposition or trial. Chapter 6 covers possible topics to discuss, depending on whether you are preparing for deposition or trial.

Assess Your Witness and Set Realistic Goals

In order to shape an individualized preparation session, you must first have an accurate assessment of what the focus of the session needs to be. This can vary from a simple explanation of what will occur, to correction of serious communication problems, to extensive Q&A practice. If you have adequately assessed your witness's communication and presentation needs, the preparation session can be tailored to what may be required in the way of assistance.

Remember that the purpose of witness preparation is re-direction, not change. It is naïve to think a person can be "changed" in a session lasting several hours. Remember, too, that the aim is to modify behavior by improving communication skills and perhaps appearance, but not to change someone's personality. Changing another person's personality is not only an inappropriate goal of witness preparation, it is likely not a realistic one.

Advise the Witness about Your Rules

Nearly every attorney has his or her own laundry list of rules for deposition and trial testimony, gleaned from work with litigation consultants or learned over years of experience preparing witnesses. If you have a list of "do and don'ts" that you want to share with the witness, now is a good time. Keep in mind, however, that verbalizing a list of rules should never substitute for substantive practice. As every parent of a teenager knows, simply telling someone not to do something is much less effective than allowing the person to make the mistake and learn from it.

If you use a list of rules to prepare your witnesses, keep the list short and concise. Rules are best learned during actual Q&A practice and when giving feedback. In those circumstances, the witness has a specific behavior to which the rule can be anchored, and it is more likely to be recalled.

Here are some of the more common basic rules provided by attorneys to their witnesses.

- Tell the truth. It is not only a rule of law and you will swear to do so, but the truth is always easiest to remember.
- Listen carefully to the question and avoid formulating an answer until you are certain that you heard and understand the question as asked, not as you wish it were asked.
- Take your time in answering questions. This is not the quiz show Jeopardy and there is no reward for answering questions quickly. Speedy answers will not make you appear more intelligent, knowledgeable or honest, and they will not end the process earlier. Rather, quick answers may make you appear impulsive, thoughtless, or careless.
- Slow down and pause before answering any question. Take time to think and mentally phrase what you want to say. Don't talk off the top of your head.
- Don't answer a question you don't understand. If the question is unclear, or if you don't understand the context, ask for clarification. You do not have to answer any question you don't clearly comprehend.
- Don't guess or estimate. If you are not absolutely certain regarding a fact, just say, "I don't know" or "I don't recall." Even if the questioner persists, don't surrender or guess in order to please him or her.
- Don't volunteer information outside the question. Be succinct. Be comfortable with silences.

- Avoid absolutes such as "never" and "always." Use of such words can lock in testimony when there are likely to be exceptions. Words such as "usually," "often," and "rarely" are more accurate.
- When asked a question related to a document, ask to see the document, read the relevant portion without speaking, ask for a repeat of the question, and then answer.
- Ask for a break after about an hour. You cannot take a break with a question pending, but breaks are encouraged to refresh and relax.

Regardless of the specific rules you choose to share with your witness, be aware that additional explanation may be needed or desired. You may also want to discuss your rules on how to handle hypothetical questions, requests to produce documents, memory lapses, or other special issues you expect to arise in the deposition or at trial.

Prepare Questions in Advance

One of the most common questions asked by witnesses is, "What are they going to ask me?" This is where Q&A practice greatly benefits the witness. Not only do they learn about the types of questions that are likely to be asked, but they have an opportunity to think through how they might respond to such questions. Many witnesses are surprised to learn, for example, that questions may be asked in a deposition that may seem irrelevant to the case issues, that attorneys representing other parties may ask questions at the deposition, or that only the opposing attorney, and not you, will likely be questioning them at a deposition.

You can never know exactly what questions opposing counsel will ask your witness, but you can anticipate many of them. What would you ask if positions were reversed? What have your experts identified as weaknesses of your case? What have you found to be problematic issues in similar cases? If you are familiar with opposing counsel's style, what questions has the attorney asked in the past in similar cases? What do you feel are the "soft spots" of your case? What will the witness have the most difficulty answering?

When preparing potential questions, you should include all types: open-ended, closed-ended, hypotheticals, questions containing false assumptions, leading questions, compound questions, "loaded" questions containing embedded assumptions or inaccuracies, questions that improperly summarize prior answers, repetitive or antagonistic questions designed to "bully" the witness, and those likely to push the witness's emotional buttons. The practice Q&A should be conceived as a worst-case scenario practice, as it is ultimately wiser to enable your witness to withstand a grueling interrogation than to be blindsided with challenging questions from a quarrelsome, aggressive attorney who lays traps and attempts to manipulate your client's testimony in order to get important concessions.

Provide Question and Answer Practice

All witnesses benefit to varying degrees from having one or more practice Q&A segments. The list of potential areas for questioning should be well thought out and prepared by the attorney in advance. Potential questions should be reviewed, with emphasis on the toughest questions the witness is likely to be asked. Shielding the witness from areas of questioning that may be uncomfortable or difficult in order to prevent arousing anxiety is a formula for disaster.

If possible and practical, use a colleague to role-play Q&A but only if the person is up to speed on the case. Instruct your client to "stay in role" so you can assess his or her ability to answer a series of questions without interruption.

If you have some awareness of the opposing attorney's style, now is a good time to share that information. Even better is to have an attorney colleague conduct the practice Q&A in that style. Since you will be teaching the witness to ignore the *way* in which a question is asked, and focus only on the *content*, attention to this detail will pay dividends later.

Limit Q&A segments to five to ten minutes each. As teachers advise, distributed practice is more helpful than massed practice. Practice for about ten minutes, and then critique that segment. Practice Q&A segments typically constitute the majority of the preparation time.

Video Record the Practice

As suggested in Chapter 3, video recording some or all of the practice Q&A sequences and playing them back can be an extremely effective learning tool. It can also help to de-sensitize a witness to the presence of a camera if the deposition is to be video recorded by opposing counsel. If you are video recording the practice session, play back the segment and allow the witness to do some of the "Monday morning quarterbacking." Self-examination and critique is considerably more effective than any feedback you may offer. If a segment has gone well, play back just enough to reinforce several exchanges that the witness handles well and encourage him or her to continue that behavior.

If the witness has a strong objection to being video recorded, and the deposition is not likely to be video recorded, it may be wise to avoid this process. The decision whether to video record is a judgment call on the part of the attorney, but most trial consultants or communications experts will highly recommend it. If video recording is done, be certain it is protected as attorney-client work product.

Give Constructive Feedback and Guidance

Not all attorneys are experts in communication. Many struggle with what advice to give their witnesses, and what advice may only further confuse a witness or elevate the anxiety level. By the same token, some people receive feedback more willingly than others. While providing guidance and suggestions is an essential part of the witness preparation process, it must be offered in a way that is most receptive. Let's look at few rules for providing feedback.

Give positive feedback first. This helps to put a witness at ease and reinforces the belief that s/he is doing something right. Witnesses will be more willing to listen to your suggestions about what needs to be improved or changed if they first hear positive comments. An example might be: "I like the way you gave the questioner good eye contact, and you could be even more effective if you would increase your volume a bit to reflect greater confidence in your answer."

Give the witness only one or two directions at a time. Here are examples of feedback that will be overwhelming and feedback that will be more helpful.

Example of Overwhelming Feedback

"Remember to look at the attorney and keep your head up. Don't use the phrase 'scared for his safety' because that sounds extreme. It would be better to use the phrase 'concerned for his safety.' And don't rock in the chair or lean back. Remember that you have to slow down and pause between the question and the answer because you are often starting to answer before the attorney has even finished his question. And don't forget the timeline we talked about last time we met. Be sure you stick with the timeline because the exact time of the accident is very important in this case."

Example of Helpful Feedback

"I like the way you kept your answer direct and to the point. Remember to use the word 'concerned' instead of 'frightened' because it is more accurate and less extreme."

Avoid excessive criticism and "nitpicking." Watch a Q&A segment through without any criticism at all. Then go back, focusing on just a few issues. Allow the witness to identify areas in which answers were less effective than they could have been. The most effective learning will occur when the witness is able to recognize listening errors and answers that could be given more precisely or more accurately. Pummeling a witness with disparagements and re-phrasing all of the witness's answers in your own language will soon become defeating for the witness.

Praise the good communication skills your client demonstrates. No client is ever all bad, and finding some communication strengths to praise is essential to avoid giving the impression the witness is hopeless. Let your client know what she is doing correctly, and what to not worry about. Focus on what behaviors and attitudes you believe will make a more effective witness. This is the time to build confidence.

Allow witnesses to speak in their own language. In practice Q&A segments, if your witness does not understand a question, or a certain term being used, ask how s/he would ask the question or what term s/he would use. This will help you understand the witness's language and thought patterns. Attempting to program a witness with the verbiage you would use to answer a question is not wise. Witnesses cannot possibly memorize your speech patterns and vocabulary. Even if this were possible, you run the risk of making the witness sound rehearsed or over-coached.

Avoid losing patience when a witness fails to follow your advice. Frustration is contagious and your client will reciprocate in kind. Be realistic. Not everyone is amenable to practice; not everyone is a good listener; not everyone is attentive and cooperative. Accept the limitations of your witness as patiently as possible.

Don't overload your client with too much detail and too much to remember. An article published in 2001 by a Midwest attorney touted "130 Rules for Every Deponent." This is too much for the average person to process and remember. Setting the expectation that a witness must remember and put into practice all of your rules and suggestions will be overwhelming and anxiety-provoking. It can become an embarrassing catastrophe as your client freezes on the stand in a desperate attempt to recall the appropriate rule. Focus on five or six key things to work on and provide a few simple guidelines. Know when enough is enough.

Provide reassurance that it is all right to be nervous. Almost all witnesses are nervous, and some nervousness is beneficial to sustain attention and effort. You may even acknowledge your own nervousness in certain situations. The last thing you want to promote is anxiety about feeling nervous!

Prepare for the Possibility of Being Called Adversely

If you anticipate that at trial your witness may be called adversely by plaintiff's counsel or the prosecutor, it is critical that you address this possibility in the preparation session. Explain what is meant by being "called adversely," and how this alters the plan for laying out the defense story to the jury. Important points to cover with the witness include:

- Opposing counsel has a purpose in mind in calling a defense witness during his or her case: to expose a witness in a negative light early in the trial, or to establish and/or highlight a key theme for the plaintiff's or prosecutor's case.
- Answering questions in this circumstance will be more challenging because the witness must attempt to make a positive first impression on jurors while being essentially "cross-examined."
- It is unlikely the witness will be asked anything in this process that s/he was not already asked in deposition (if one was taken).
- The questioning will likely be more limited in scope (an explanation why this is so may be given if it does not become too complex).

- The defense story is best told when the defense presents its case and you are conducting a direct examination of the witness; if possible, answers provided under adverse circumstances should be succinct and responsive.
- Attempts to give more complete explanations to questions asked under adverse circumstances are more likely to be viewed by jurors as defensive or argumentative.
- It will be challenging to restrain oneself when answering questions under adverse circumstances, but the defense story is best told when the defense puts on its case, and it is unlikely a witness will be given the opportunity for lengthy explanations anyway.
- Highlight how "adverse" testimony is much like a deposition, only better, because you will also be able to question them, allowing for additional explanations or corrections to misstatements (although no new evidence or testimony can be introduced).

When working with a confident witness who may be anxious to tell his or her story under adverse conditions, it is helpful to suggest some ways to respond when opposing counsel wants to limit an answer, or when the witness is tempted to give a "Yes, but..." explanation. The following examples might be suggested to the witness:

> *"Yes, I did send the memo directly after the meeting, for several good reasons."*
>
> *"I did position myself directly under the suspect's window, and I'm happy to explain why I did that."*

These answers will likely satisfy the "Just answer yes or no" admonishment, but at the same time plant a seed that there is more to the story, to be told at a later time, or that there is a more complete answer. In the best of circumstances, the witness will be invited by opposing counsel to give a further explanation, without sounding defensive. If no opportunity is given, the jurors will expect to hear more of this witness's testimony at a later time.

Teach the Importance of Listening

Good attorneys know the best witnesses listen attentively to the question being asked, exactly as it is being asked. Most people pride themselves on being good listeners, but the skills required in most day-to-day conversations are different from those needed at a deposition or trial. Most witnesses are unaware of the difference because it is not every day they are called upon to give sworn testimony. In ordinary conversation, people understand what the other person *means* or is trying to say, not the actual words used. We *interpret* what is being said or asked in a larger context that lends meaning to the conversation. This is why many witnesses may hear a question they do not fully understand, then mentally massage it within a broader context, and answer the interpreted version. This process enhances the flow of social conversation, but it can be a recipe for disaster under oath.

Teach witnesses that when giving testimony at a deposition or trial, the actual *words* must be the focus because every word has significance—it is being transcribed! This can be difficult for witnesses to grasp because they are not accustomed to this level of listening, and active listening does not come naturally.

Active Listening

How does active listening differ from just listening? Active listening requires full attention on the questioner, and to what he or she is asking. It requires focusing on the entirety of what is being asked, and making sure there is clear understanding of what it is the questioner wants to know. An example is the everyday question, "How are you?" Most people listen and answer this question according to what they think the other person wants to know: "I'm busy at work" or "I'm not feeling very well." They rarely attempt to clarify a mutual understanding by asking if the other person means physically, financially, spiritually, or emotionally. In a legal setting, however, it is exactly that level of understanding that should be registered before a witness can give a responsive answer.

One of the most common interferences with active listening is prematurely focusing on the answer. Communication specialists refer to this as "out-listening." Teach witnesses how to overcome this tendency in the Q&A practice. Here are some techniques that have proven effective:

- Force the witness to count to five before giving an answer, as this forces the separation of listening from formulating an answer.
- Have the witness repeat the question as it was asked before giving the answer, an exercise that can be enlightening to witnesses who see themselves as competent listeners.
- Suggest the witness incorporate part of the question in the answer, a practice that compels the person to mentally repeat the question.

Teaching witnesses to be "expert listeners" takes considerable practice. Don't skip this important aspect of the preparation, as it is the most critical element of effective testimony. Becoming expert listeners will make it nearly impossible for opposing counsel to control their testimony, put words in their mouth, or entrap them with embedded assumptions or other inaccuracies.

Teach the Importance of Thinking Before Speaking

Many witnesses operate under the false assumption that what first comes to mind is the best answer. Just the opposite is often the case. Teach your witness that there are five steps to answering questions:

1. Listen
2. Pause
3. Think
4. Answer
5. Stop talking

Practice this pace until you are satisfied the witness has internalized the steps. If necessary, take the questioning precisely one step at a time: state the question, ask the witness to repeat the question, hold up your hand until the witness has taken time to pause and think, summon the witness to give the answer, and then hold up your hand again as a signal to stop talking. It will be awkward at first, but it will demonstrate for the witness very specifically what the pace should be. Make certain the pace becomes habituated. If during later questioning the witness fails to follow the steps, merely holding up your hand will be a reminder.

Provide Guidance on Response Length

It is unwise to advise a witness to attempt to answer opposing counsel's questions in a deposition with "yes," "no," or "I don't know." While you may think you are preventing your witness from making a harmful admission, this is simply poor advice. It cannot and should not be followed. Here are just a few reasons why one-word answers are ineffective:

1. This is discovery. Chances are low that opposing counsel will limit questions to those that can be answered with simple agreement or disagreement. Opposing counsel wants to hear your witness talk and explain. Part of his or her assessment is how well your witness communicates, as well as the degree of confidence the witness demonstrates when answering questions.

2. If opposing counsel asks questions that can be answered by simple agreement or disagreement, chances are high they contain critical false or erroneous assumptions that, left unchecked, can mischaracterize important testimony. To correct such errors, it is essential for your witness to speak in his or her own words.

3. If the case proceeds to trial, your witness will likely be called to the stand to explain important facts and events. If the deposition transcript is filled with one-word answers, but your witness is now able to provide important context and details, jurors are left wondering why this information was not provided at the deposition.

4. A simple "yes," "no," or "I don't know" is rarely a complete and honest answer. While no one would suggest that a witness volunteer information outside the question, even the most obvious questions often beg some qualifier. Consider this question: "Shouldn't a manufacturer do everything possible to ensure the safety of its product?" It would be difficult to disagree. However, a qualifier might certainly be in order: "A manufacturer has a responsibility to do everything they can to assure the reasonable safety of its product, but it is not possible to anticipate all the ways in which it might be misused."

5. Witnesses who limit their responses to one-word answers rarely make a good impression on judges, opposing attorneys, or jurors.

The best rule on response length is to speak succinctly, but with enough context to make the answer complete and accurate. Consider the following example in which there are two possible answers—a simple one and a complete one. Judge for yourself which one is most truthful and effective.

Which Is Better?

Q: Ms. Smith, on the afternoon of January 4, you failed to stop at the red light on the corner of Fifth and Adams Streets when you smashed into the left side of my client's Toyota, didn't you? Just answer my question.

A#1: Yes.

A#2: There was ice on the roadway, so even though I tried, I was not able to stop at the red light.

The witness who had been advised to say "yes" or "no" in response to questions would not be as effective as the witness who gave A#2. Teaching a witness the distinction between a one-word answer and a succinct but complete answer will make the difference between an ineffective and an effective truth-teller.

Suggest "Safe Harbors"

Nearly every witness, at one point in a deposition or trial, will be at a loss for words. A responsive answer simply cannot be formulated, for any number of reasons. When this occurs, a witness may wish for a life jacket or a safe harbor to protect them from an answer that could pull them under or out into deeper waters.

Examples of "Safe Harbors"

- *"It depends on the situation."*
- *"I've given the best, most honest answer I can give on that issue."*
- *"That question doesn't make sense to me. Can you ask it differently?"*
- *"I'm not certain and I don't want to guess or speculate."*

- *"I've never been asked that question before. I'll need a moment to think about it."*
- *"I don't know the answer."*
- *"I don't recall that [incident] with clarity."*
- *"That falls outside my area of expertise."*

The idea is to assure the witness that not all questions may be capable of being answered, or of being answered as asked. Safe harbors should be used judiciously and never used as a means of dodging a difficult question.

Provide Guidance on Demeanor and Courtroom Conduct

If you are preparing a witness for deposition, make certain s/he is aware of proper clothing, grooming, and demeanor. This is especially important if the witness's deposition is to be videotaped. Even if no videotaping is expected, the witness needs to make a positive impression on the opposing attorney, who is likely evaluating the witness's "jury appeal" if the case goes to trial. Advise the witness to sit up straight, look at the attorney, and appear eager to answer questions and tell the truth. Discuss any distracting gestures or facial grimaces to be avoided.

If you are preparing a witness for a hearing or trial, also be certain to discuss appropriate courtroom dress, grooming, and demeanor. If the witness is a party who will be seated beside you throughout the trial, explain the importance of being attentive at all times. Parties who slump in their chairs, doodle, appear distracted or sleepy, or seem preoccupied with some other activity have been criticized in post-verdict interviews by jurors who viewed such behaviors as evidence of indifference or disrespect. Discuss the importance of appropriate conduct outside the courtroom, as a juror could be within earshot or in a position to observe behaviors that might reflect badly on the witness. During the trial a witness must be warned to make absolutely no contact with a juror, whether inside or outside the courthouse.

Make certain your witness knows that when on the witness stand at a jury trial, orientation (and eye contact) when giving an explanatory answer should be directed toward the jurors, not the attorney or the judge. Jurors tend to distrust witnesses who cannot "look them in the eye." Instruct your witness that when taking the witness stand, the chair itself should be angled slightly toward the jury box. In this way, the witness can observe the polite gesture of looking to the attorney for the question, but direct the answer to the jurors, without appearing to be watching a tennis match. You can also assist by positioning yourself at the far corner of the jury box (if allowed) so your witness's eye contact need not be divided.

Acknowledge that while looking at jurors can be difficult when one is nervous, it is important for a witness to give some eye contact to jurors, particularly when responding to key questions, so that jurors can judge the credibility of the answer given. It is not necessary, however, to direct every answer to the jurors, as this could appear coached and unnatural. The idea is to orient the witness in the direction of the jury box, making eye contact a little easier.

End the Session on a Positive Note

Be mindful of the point in time when your witness has reached his or her "absorption limit" and end the session. It is often better to schedule a second session than to risk overwhelming the witness in a single one.

Re-cap the essential points and what was learned. Ask the witness to verbalize the key points she or he learned in the session, and to list the specific communication elements that need reinforcement over the next day or two. Provide "homework" if the witness needs to continue some aspect of the practice (e.g., allowing opposing counsel to complete a question before beginning a response, slowing the pace of communication, etc.). Encourage the witness to practice specific skills (e.g., active listening, succinct responding, pausing before speaking) when communicating with family and colleagues over the next few days.

Make certain the witness has all of the documents and records about which s/he will be questioned. Instruct the witness that these must be thoroughly reviewed so as to be very familiar with them, but that memorization is neither possible nor required. Reassure your witness that testifying is like an open book examination and all records and documents will be available for reference at deposition or trial if needed.

Explain the need to set aside undisturbed time for records review, indicate how much time you expect to be devoted to the review, and inquire when s/he plans to review them. Don't be surprised to hear that the witness will "spend a few minutes with them before the deposition or trial." If you feel this will be inadequate, say so. Then describe your expectations and develop a specific plan for reviewing records and documents. No one should know your witness's records, memos, e-mails, or documents better than the witness him or herself.

Determine if another session is needed. If so, explain your reasoning and get the cooperation of the witness. If several sessions are anticipated, schedule them several days or a week apart, to allow time for "incubation" between sessions.

Make certain your witness knows the location and time for the deposition or start of trial. Don't assume s/he has given their participation as much importance as you do. If necessary, make certain an assistant provides a reminder the day before. An ounce of prevention is worth a ton of headaches. Instruct your witness not to bring anything to a deposition or to court that you have not specifically instructed the witness to bring.

A Courtroom Visit May Be Warranted

The courtroom can be a daunting place—sterile, formal, and cold. Whenever possible, take your witness to an actual courtroom. This may be particularly helpful if your witness has never before been in a courtroom and his or her testimony is critical in the case. Once when working with a group of hospital-based nurses who were uniformly very frightened about testifying in court, the attorney located an empty courtroom and obtained permission to use it for a few hours. Asking the nurses to meet at the courtroom gave them an opportunity to learn the driving directions, locate the parking area, and find the appropriate room. Each nurse was [mock] sworn in and given the opportunity to sit in the witness chair to answer a few direct and cross-examination questions. They were guided in how to position the witness chair so they could look at (or in the direction of) the jurors. The benefit of this exercise was immeasurable. The de-sensitization effect of having been in the witness chair in a courtroom helped the nurses control anxiety and testify with more confidence than they otherwise might have.

If it is not possible to make a training visit to the courtroom, you might arrange a "sit in" at another time. When a witness is also a party in the lawsuit and sitting with you at counsel table, have him or her sit in the witness chair and practice getting questions and giving answers to the jury box during a lunch break or at the end of the day before the witness will be called.

When Assistance from a Consultant Is Indicated

With some help and assistance from an attorney, most people can become good witnesses. However, every attorney has encountered the witness who seems unresponsive to sound advice and for whom no amount of preparation seems to help. For example, imagine that despite two practice sessions, your client still refuses to stay on point and answer a direct question. Or you may have become frustrated in trying to help your client keep answers shorter and you are having nightmares she will say something inappropriate or harmful at her deposition. Or you are uncomfortable with telling your client he must cut his hair and shave off an unkempt beard. This may be the time to call for reinforcements in the way of a professional trial consultant.

At other times, you may simply not "connect" with a witness. For whatever reason, the two of you seem to bring out the worst in each other and practice sessions dissolve into arguments and annoyance on both sides. You question the witness's truthfulness or feel disrespected by a lack of attentiveness. Attorneys tend to be logical thinkers who organize their thoughts and then express them in articulate ways. This is not true for most witnesses. Many people have difficulty expressing themselves, actively avoid debate, and rarely have to defend their actions to strangers. When these two modes of thinking and communication clash, the result can be frustration on both sides.

Occasionally, an attorney simply wants to avoid any threat to the sound rapport established with the client and feels uncomfortable posing challenging or intimidating questions to that person. This may be the time to call in a professional trial consultant, and to consider using a colleague to pose potential deposition or cross-examination questions during the preparation session.

A trial consultant, litigation psychologist, or communications specialist, particularly one experienced in the kind of litigation you are managing (e.g., professional negligence, personal injury, securities fraud), is a professional who specializes in preparing witnesses for depositions, hearings, and trials. He or she should be able to handle most of the typical problems that are encountered with witnesses. The consultant can assist in teaching your client how to listen more carefully, to modify a belligerent attitude, to speak up or slow down, to improve focus, to give more succinct answers, and to be a more effective truth teller. There are limits, of course, on what can be improved in a session lasting only a few hours, so expectations have to be reasonable. Only you and the consultant can determine whether additional sessions will yield additional benefits.

Lastly, a trial consultant brings a different perspective to the witness preparation session than does the attorney. The consultant observes and judges the witness through the eyes of jurors. Most consultants have extensive experience in interviewing actual jurors after trials to learn how various courtroom behaviors and communication styles affect witness believability and credibility. Most are removed from the case and more objective regarding a witness's potential impact on jurors. At times, only an outsider can vocalize what the attorneys or others in the trial team may be thinking, such as, "This witness is telling the truth, but he doesn't act like it." This important benefit alone may be worth the modest cost. (See Chapter 10 for suggestions on how to locate a consultant in your area.)

A Reading Resource May Be Helpful

Witnesses often ask if there is anything available they can take home to refresh themselves or to expand upon what they have learned. You might consider purchasing a supply of *Handbook for Witnesses*, also authored by Dodge and Ryan, to provide to your witnesses as a helpful guide. (See Appendix C for ordering information.)

CHAPTER 8

MATTERS OF MEMORY AND RECALL

One of the most prevalent concerns of many witnesses is fear that their memories will fail them when they are being asked questions at a deposition, hearing, or trial. Like most of us, witnesses can have difficulty recalling events and details that occurred months or even years earlier. An important role of any attorney in preparing a witness is to assist the client with these real concerns.

Enhancing Memory and Recall by Replaying Events

A witness giving testimony at a deposition or at trial is actually involved in a complex mental activity in which there are many opportunities for error. Since witnesses are describing their *memories* of events, there are three areas of potential error:

1. The witness's original *observation* of the event may have been faulty (time of day, lighting, position, fatigue, familiarity, etc.).
2. The *memory* itself may be inaccurate.
3. The *description* of the memory may be inaccurate or misleading.

Compared to most animals, the human powers of sense (sight, smell, and hearing) are limited. Human memory is fallible. Even in perfect conditions, there are few people who can produce a memory precisely and impartially. Given the vast amount of time that has likely passed between the event at issue and the date of the testimony, the mind can begin to add components to memory in order to make it compatible with the most favorable recollection of events.

Add to this the fact that not everything that goes into the brain is equally susceptible to recall. The brain acts as a censor of some unpleasant experiences (accident victims cannot recall how the accident actually happened); the brain "edits" memory. Relevance is also a factor. The brain involuntarily eliminates trivial detail or irrelevant information; sometimes the brain condenses memory. The trouble is that trivial details can gain importance later. For example, we may not recall our automobile license plate number even though we may see it many times a week because our brain knows it can be retrieved easily at any time. But if our car is stolen, it becomes very important to recall it quickly. Lastly, fact and fancy are often intermingled and what is recalled often contains some wish-fulfillment. That is, memory is susceptible to selective factors and to distortion.

The reconstruction of an experience in words nearly always involves some distortion: words have shades of meaning; simultaneous events can become superimposed, a person's vocabulary and powers of description vary considerably. Sometimes the association of ideas with particular words is different in the witness from the association made by the listener (e.g., descriptors such as stressful, cruel, painful, rude, weak, fast, big, frightening). Enhancing memory and recall by reviewing documents, creating a basic timeline, and providing opportunities for the witness to express recollections is an essential part of the preparation session.

Reviewing Documents and Potential Areas of Questioning

No witness should go to a deposition, hearing or trial without a general outline of what he or she is likely to be asked. One of the most important goals of pre-deposition or pre-trial preparation is to review records and documents about which the witness is likely to be questioned, and to outline potential areas of testimony. This helps to refresh the witness's memory and assists in thinking through potential responses. It also reduces the witness's anxiety about being surprised by a forgotten or overlooked document or record. When years have passed between the incidents involved in the lawsuit, and the actual witness examination, faded memories can be common. Refreshing memories is a critical aspect of witness preparation. Reviewing documents, records, and a timeline of events is much like remembering the details of a past vacation by looking at the photos taken at the time—they spark memories not otherwise recalled.

Preparing a Timeline of Events

One effective means of refreshing a witness's memory is to assist him or her in constructing a basic timeline of events: What happened first? On what date? Then what occurred? Often the witness's story begins before the actual events in question, and it often ends after the last occurrence. For example, the story may actually begin with the weather turning bad, the choice of a particular door lock, the referral of a patient to a specific medical specialist, or the decision to issue company stock. When a witness is key to the telling of the case story, it is critical that he or she not only know where the story begins and ends, but the point at which certain testimony becomes relevant. The mere creation of a timeline often stimulates memory, solidifies recollections, and leads to the development of case themes.

Using the "Four Drawers" of Memory

Every witness should be made aware of the "four drawers" of memory. Explain that they can think of the source for answering questions as a file cabinet with four drawers. Any of the four drawers may be opened in order to answer a question.

The Four Memory Drawers

Unassisted Memory

Refreshed Memory

Routines and Habits

"I don't recall" or "I don't know"

Unassisted memory includes those events and details that are easily retrieved from memory. They are recalled because they had special significance, such as the design of one's wedding gown, the name of the doctor who delivered one's baby thirty years ago, or the intersection where a bad accident occurred. These details are recalled because they remain accessible in memory regardless of the passage of time.

Refreshed memory, however, requires a cue to stimulate recall. A person might not remember what they received for their eighth birthday, but if shown a photo from the family album in which they are beaming beside a new red bicycle, the recall would be enhanced with details of the party. A nurse may not recall the details of a procedure she performed on a patient three years earlier until she looked at the medical records and re-read her notes about the procedure. A manager may have forgotten the content of a specific e-mail sent several years ago to an employee until it is shown to him. Memories thought to be inaccessible may be brought back to consciousness by reviewing documents, discussing a timeline of events, or simply exposing oneself to cues that might bring the memory back to light. However, while it is perfectly acceptable for a witness to *refresh* memory by reviewing records, discussing events with you, or mentally re-staging relevant incidents, it is never acceptable to *re-create* them or to allow anyone else to do so for the witness.

Routines and habits are those behaviors or thoughts we engage in automatically or so frequently that they become subconscious. We may not recall the name of the street at which we stopped for the red light, but we are certain we stopped because that is what we do when we see a red light. A doctor may not have a specific recollection of scrubbing and gloving her hands before a surgery, but she knows this was done because it is part of her professional pre-surgical routine. It is not always necessary to have a specific recall if we are certain we engaged in a behavior or made a certain judgment because it is part of an ingrained habit or practice.

Not remembering or knowing the answer to a question is not a weakness. A cardinal rule for answering questions that rely on memory is never to allow your witness to be pushed to recall more than s/he actually does. Remind the witness that the fourth drawer is the empty one—it contains no certain memory. Most people feel apologetic or guilty about absent or imperfect memory. The natural tendency is to "fill in" memory gaps with speculation or guessing. This can be a serious error in a legal context. Remind the witness to focus on what s/he *does* remember, and not to worry about what cannot be recalled. If the memory is incomplete or unclear, explain that it is perfectly acceptable to say simply, "I don't remember" or "I don't have a clear memory and I don't want to guess" or "I don't know the answer to that question." There is no need to offer an apology. It can be difficult for witnesses to use the "I-don't-remember" drawer because they assume that if a question is asked, they must generate an answer, even if memory fails them and nothing helps to refresh their memory. They don't want to disappoint you or the questioner, and they do not want to appear to be hiding information or dodging a difficult question. Give the witness permission to admit they don't know or don't recall.

CHAPTER 9

SPECIAL WITNESS CHALLENGES

Because of certain personality characteristics, past bad legal experiences, language barriers, age, intelligence, or other factors, some witnesses will pose special challenges in preparing them for a deposition, hearing, or trial. We cannot address all the unusual situations you may encounter, but below is a discussion of some of the more common ones we have encountered.

The "I Know Everything" Witness

Some witnesses believe they know a great deal about the events or issues in the lawsuit, and may end up answering questions about issues with which they actually have very limited knowledge and experience. Corporate executives, physicians, scientists, skilled technicians, and seasoned nurses often fall into this category. Their answers may conflict with the testimony of others, such as experts in the field or people more familiar with the issue. This can be damaging.

Preparation of the "I know everything" witness should focus on restricting the witness's answers. Some attorneys refer to this as "staying inside your box" and not speculating outside one's area of expertise and familiarity. You may need to make a point by purposely trapping such witnesses with questions that demonstrate their lack of knowledge. Give these witnesses reassurance that they are not expected to know everything, to answer every question posed to them, or to have an opinion on every aspect of the case issues. Caution them not to engage opposing counsel in a discussion or debate in order to make a point. This can be a destructive trap. Knowing when to stop talking is just as vital as knowing when to start.

The "I Know Nothing" Witness

Advising a witness to give short answers is usually good advice, but advising a witness to aim for answering "yes," "no," or "I don't know" to as many questions as possible is poor advice. At trial, such witnesses appear uninformed, uncooperative, or unintelligent. There is a big difference between being succinct and giving a responsive answer, and being guarded, tight-lipped, and obstinate. The witness who believes that a one-word response speeds up the process and reduces the anxiety of speaking in public will soon find that opposing counsel is happy to speak for them.

Improving an "I know nothing" witness can sometimes be as simple as giving them permission to answer questions completely. Some witnesses have previously been coached to say only yes or no, and they are merely attempting to follow the same rule. Re-orient them to current thinking about witness effectiveness and give them the green light to speak.

For some tight-lipped or overly anxious witnesses, Q&A practice will be particularly important. Modeling what is meant by a complete answer will help them understand what is expected and encouraged. Practice, along with positive reinforcement, will also help to reduce anxiety and build confidence.

The Self-Centered Witness

It seems safe to say that among the qualities people usually find endearing and attractive, self-centeredness is not high on the list. A brash, arrogant, self-promoting personality is a turn-off, and a difficult person to prepare as a witness. Among psychologists, such people are often referred to as narcissists, egocentrics, or self-absorbed personalities. Characteristics of these personality types that pose preparation challenges to any attorney or consultant include the following:

- An obvious self-focus in interpersonal exchanges
- Lack of psychological awareness and personal insight (i.e., low self-monitoring)
- Difficulty feeling or expressing empathy
- Hypersensitivity to insults (real or imagined) and difficulty accepting feedback or guidance
- Pretending to be more important than they really are
- Bragging and exaggerating their accomplishments
- Claiming to be an "expert" at many things and to have had nearly every experience imaginable
- Using distortion, illusion, and projection to blame others when things have gone wrong
- Inability to see someone else's perspective

Self-centered witnesses tend to be particularly low self-monitors, and special approaches are often necessary in order to prepare them for deposition or trial. Following are some techniques that we have found to be effective.

Allow some venting. Despite their egotistical demeanor, these witnesses can actually be vulnerable and insecure. Invite such witnesses to share their concerns and frustrations before launching immediately into the communication practice. You may be surprised at what lies beneath the brash exterior.

Couch your feedback somewhat differently. To avoid rejection of communication suggestions and feedback by an egotistical witness, it may be necessary to use a non-threatening preface, such as "You will be even more effective if you say..." or "Your juror appeal will be much increased if you..." Trial consultant Douglas Keene suggests self-absorbed witnesses must be "redirected," not corrected. For example, assuring such witnesses that their goal at trial is to educate jurors rather than to explain or argue with the attorneys can redirect their frame of reference. The criterion for an effective answer then becomes, "Would a tenth grader understand what you are describing?" rather than "That answer won't be effective."

Use their ideas. Narcissists may be challenging to prepare as witnesses, but they are also often intelligent and articulate. They may have insightful ideas that can be developed into case themes and trial strategies. Don't allow your annoyance with a self-centered witness to block your openness to ideas that may have considerable merit.

Don't lecture. You should be doing very little talking in preparation sessions with egotistical witnesses. Lectures and explanations are of no value to such witnesses, as they will be focused merely on finding loopholes with which to argue and prove they are right and you are wrong. Instead of talking, focus on Q&A practice, as this will be most productive. Narcissists learn best when they become their own critics. Allow them to give themselves feedback and critique their own responses. Play to their strengths by allowing them to demonstrate to you their insights into their own communication patterns.

The Overly Timid or Overly Aggressive Witness

Although we have rarely encountered an extremely timid or overly aggressive witness, colleagues have suggested a technique that appears to be effective in helping these witnesses become more effective. With a very timid or overly compliant witness, they suggest having the person "role play" how they would expect a very timid witness to respond to questions. Practice with a variety of questions, and encourage the person to act as submissive and shy as possible. This exercise will sensitize them to how others may view their style of responding, and will enable them to see how effectiveness is diminished when a witness is overly shy or timid.

The same exercise can help with overly aggressive, loud, and angry witnesses. Having them "role play" the vocal and physical behavior of an overly aggressive person enables the witness to see how similar their own behavior is to the role-played scenarios. Often this exercise can result in an "a-ha" moment when the witness sees their own behavior reflected back.

Preparing Expert Witnesses

The best expert is not always the best expert money can buy. Credentials are important to jurors, along with whether the expert has a local versus a national reputation. Experts who are actively participating in the profession are typically more influential than those drug out of moth balls. A strong sense of self-confidence, without appearing egotistical, and some experience in teaching or mentoring are also extremely helpful.

The most common method of expert witness preparation is self-preparation, and there are several excellent books on the market designed to help expert witnesses prepare themselves for deposition or trial testimony. Perhaps the best-known and most prolific expert on preparing expert witnesses is Stanley L. Brodsky, and his self-help books can be located easily on any Internet bookseller site, such as Amazon.com. His best-known guidebooks, along with other resources for preparing experts in various fields are listed in Appendix C.

In addition to self-help, expert witnesses can benefit from the same witness-centered preparation sessions as fact witnesses. Attorneys have a vested interest in having their experts appear credible and believable to the jurors they are attempting to influence. In "expert versus expert" contests, the most influential expert is almost always the best juror educator. While credentials are important, and current employment in the field is essential, post-verdict interviews indicate that jurors pay less attention to educational credentials than they do to the expert's case-related experience and his or her ability to help them understand technical evidence without intimidating jargon or condescending simplifications.

Preparation of experts must take into account the intellectual ability of jurors to understand complicated technical aspects of the case, and their desire to do so. This means the expert must be able to demonstrate her or his expertise, but use common analogies and simplified terms that the ordinary person can comprehend. In post-trial interviews, it is not uncommon to hear jurors report, "All that testimony about BOIs and equitization went way over my head. I got lost in the jargon." On the other hand, they do not appreciate being "talked down to." Following a medical negligence case, one juror remarked, "The expert kept referring to bowel contents as 'poop.' Did he think he was talking to a group of second-graders? It was insulting."

A question asked frequently of expert witnesses is, "You are being paid for your testimony here today, aren't you?" To which many experts honestly but unfortunately reply, "Yes, I am." Unless bribery is involved, no expert is paid for *testimony*. The more effective answer to that common question is, "I'm being paid for my time. My testimony is my own." Most jurors are aware that experts on both sides are being paid, but allowing opposing counsel to suggest their testimony is bought and paid for can impact the expert's credibility. Alert your experts to this somewhat tricky question.

Preparing Physician Witnesses

One might think doctors will most certainly be good witnesses. They are intelligent, well-educated, articulate, and usually relate well to others. And it is for those reasons that many attorneys tend to assume a physician will not require pre-deposition or pre-trial preparation. This is a risky assumption to make. In fact, the world of medicine and the legal arena couldn't be more different. Medicine involves collaborative problem-solving and a team environment in which doctors are highly respected; their decisions and explanations are rarely challenged. The legal arena is about finding fault and assigning blame, and doctor defendants will find themselves being criticized and confronted. It is a strange and frightening environment, and one in which they are ill-prepared to participate in an adversarial process.

Doctors are also accustomed to being in control. When faced with a lawsuit alleging they have essentially violated the Hippocratic Oath and harmed a patient, they may feel their control slipping away. They are not accustomed to having their judgment questioned, their medical charts examined with a microscope, and their practices challenged by an expert who in most cases has never seen the patient. Contrary to the physician's expectations, the questioning attorney is not likely to simply accept their answer, nod approvingly, gather up his or her notes, and withdraw the lawsuit.

The preparation of a physician witness must focus on giving the physician some control over his or her testimony. This can only be done through careful, thorough preparation. Some medical malpractice insurers require that all their policyholders, when named as a defendant in a negligence lawsuit, be well prepared not only for trial, but for the deposition. While they can be challenging to prepare, most defendant physicians find such preparation sessions helpful and productive. Some admit they would have been disasters as witnesses without preparation, and their attorneys agree.

While their testimony can be critical in a medical negligence case, emotion, ego, loss of control, and professional embarrassment can all affect the effectiveness of a doctor witness. For these reasons, many attorneys use professional litigation consultants to assist them in getting doctors ready for deposition and trial. There are also publications that address the special needs of this witness population. (See Appendix C for resources, including a book written by one of the authors of this handbook.)

Preparing Witnesses with Speech or Language Barriers

A witness who speaks with a heavy accent, has difficulty understanding English, or who suffers an obvious speech impediment such as stuttering or lisping poses an additional challenge. When working with those who speak heavily accented English or do not speak English well, forcing the witness to speak very slowly and to exaggerate the articulation of words will be helpful. At trial, it may be necessary to remind your witness to slow down "so jurors can hear and understand you better." If the witness also has difficulty understanding English, consider using a translator. It may be cumbersome to do so, but that must be weighed against the risk of misunderstanding questions and thus giving misleading answers.

There is little that can be done to improve the speech of a witness who suffers an impediment such as stuttering. Even speech therapists have found no fast cure. There are, however, two actions an attorney can take to assist such a witness:

1. Anxiety and nervousness typically exacerbate speech impediments. Help the witness to manage his or her anxiety by using preparation methods already discussed: reduce the unknowns, provide ample practice, and encourage the witness to keep a slow pace.
2. At trial, prepare jurors during Opening Statement by explaining that your witness has a speech impediment that cannot be overcome and which often gets amplified under conditions of stress, such as at trial. Ask jurors for their patience and understanding. This alone will have a miraculous effect.

Preparing a Criminal Defendant

In criminal matters, the defendant-witness has a constitutional right not to be forced to testify against him or herself. While a criminal defendant can, of course, willingly say something incriminating, s/he cannot be forced to do so. The witness can almost always refuse to answer a question on the grounds that the answer could be incriminating. People can be reluctant to exercise this right because of how it may be viewed by jurors. To jurors, "pleading the Fifth" can sometimes signal inherent guilt or the fear of having his or her guilt exposed through cross-examination. They wonder, "If the defendant is really innocent, why doesn't s/he testify and tell his or her side of the story?"

Many criminal defense attorneys are reluctant to put a defendant-witness on the stand, and generally this seems to make good sense, particularly if the risks outweigh the advantages of doing so. For this reason, criminal defendants are rarely prepared by their attorneys to give testimony. However, when faced with a situation in which the jury wants or needs to hear from the defendant directly, or the defendant wants to testify and the attorney has decided that there are advantages to doing so, defendant witnesses may require significant pre-trial preparation.

As with any witness, your decision about whether to put a criminal defendant on the stand should begin with an assessment of the person's ability to express him or herself. This assessment must go beyond how articulate or knowledgeable the witness appears. The issue is how the person will come across to jurors. Does he or she appear to be untruthful, evasive, or argumentative? Does the witness's demeanor and body language suggest s/he is trying to hide something? Does the person appear smug, cynical, self-righteous, or "cold and hard"? A witness who appears to be lying, even if telling the truth, can significantly damage a case.

On the other hand, a witness who might at first sight appear fearsome and threatening may actually come across well when questioned. Years ago, when working on a case involving Hell's Angels motorcycle riders, one of the most effective witnesses was a burly, bearded, and grizzled gang member. After pre-trial preparation for several hours of testimony and cross-examination, he was reported by jurors in a post-verdict interview to be completely disarming in comparison to what they had expected. They not only believed him, some described him as a "teddy bear."

The point is that if you and/or the defendant-witness are considering the risks and benefits of taking the stand in a criminal trial, a candid assessment of your witness should follow the same steps as with any other witness. What are the person's communication strengths and weaknesses? How is s/he likely to come across to jurors? Will the witness hold up under rigorous cross-examination? How confident or fearful is the witness when considering whether to testify on his or her own behalf? What will be gained or lost if the witness takes the Fifth?

CHAPTER 10

Dealing with Emotional Needs

Attorneys often feel unprepared to counsel witnesses who are overly anxious, extremely angry, or in some other way hampered in their ability to be effective witnesses. Yet many witnesses bring strong emotional states with them to preparation sessions and to depositions and trial. As an attorney, you will need to be sensitive to the emotional needs of your witness and also understand what you can provide and what may require intervention by a counselor or specialized consultant.

Emotional Issues Attorneys Often Encounter

Most witnesses arrive at a preparation session with some anxiety and fear about what is expected of them, what role they are to play in the legal process, how well they will perform, how important their testimony is to the winning of the case, how their families will cope with a lost case, how friends and colleagues will perceive their involvement in a legal battle, and a host of other concerns. Some people are able to compartmentalize so that the impending legal battle can be addressed when necessary but does not interfere with work and family life. Others find it difficult or nearly impossible to think of much else, and preoccupation with the impending trial has promoted insomnia, stomach upset, prolonged anxiety, relationship strain, and even loss of appetite and weight.

As a trial attorney, you can expect to face a gamut of emotions as you work with clients and witnesses. Those that seem to require the most sensitivity on your part include:

- Being involved in a lawsuit is what you do every day, but it is *foreign to most people*. Their emotions can run the gamut—feelings of betrayal, disbelief, anger, resentment, fear, embarrassment, anxiety, annoyance, or mistrust. Feelings of stark terror one month can be replaced by unrealistic optimism the next. Indifference at an initial meeting can transform into extreme tension as the deposition nears. As the lawsuit proceeds, expect some variation in emotional responses. This is fairly normal.

- The stress of an unfortunate incident, followed by a frightening and expensive legal entanglement is an *emotional one-two punch*. The resurgence of unpleasant memories during your witness preparation can trigger negative emotions. Be sensitive to these realities. Allow some venting by being a good listener.

- Lawsuits can take a long time to resolve and keep parties on an *emotional roller coaster*. Just when the stress of the lawsuit has receded from day-to-day life, the witness receives a letter from you or some case materials to read, and anxiety is rekindled. Although attorneys live with the ups-and-downs of lawsuit progress, this kind of unpredictable stress is particularly difficult for witnesses. Letting your client know that you are sympathetic to this effect will help build understanding and rapport.

- Lawsuits are *adversarial* and it is not unusual for a witness or client to feel alone and defensive. Remind the witness that you are part of a team that is devoted to advocating for his or her case. An ounce of reassurance will be paid back with considerable trust and confidence in you.

- Anxiety levels are often escalated by internal, often unconscious repetition of negative thoughts. It is rarely sufficient to suggest that a witness simply "think positive." Encourage the witness to remain optimistic and *avoid negative self-talk* that leads to depression and anxiety. Ask the witness to repeat the sentences that characterize his or her most negative thinking about the case. Suggest alternatives that are more positive and help to build confidence. For example:

> *Negative thought: "I'm such an idiot. I should have known better. If I had acted differently, none of this would have happened."*
>
> *New thought: "I did what I thought was right at the time. I tried my best. I couldn't foresee what would happen."*

- Encourage an overly anxious, depressed, or traumatized witness to seek *professional counseling*. Don't be hesitant to suggest that the witness may need a support person or a sounding board to help them through the lawsuit. The person may have been involved in events that led to the death of another, and the lawsuit is a constant reminder of the loss. You might be surprised to learn that although people may be given advice repeatedly by friends and spouses, they often act on it only when the same advice is given by someone they consider a professional. If professional services are needed, assist them to find an appropriate and qualified counselor.

When the Special Expertise of a Trial Consultant May Be Needed

Consider using a litigation psychologist or a trial consultant with a background in psychology and communications to assist with the preparation of a witness that you anticipate will have strong feelings of anxiety, anger, resentment, or depression as a consequence of having to give testimony at a deposition or trial. These specialized professionals can often offer assistance that an attorney feels ill-equipped to provide, thus avoiding any awkward disruption of the attorney-client relationship. Sometimes the best-heeded advice comes from an objective third party who has no stake in the eventual outcome of the case except to assist the witness to do the best job possible. Such specialized professionals also can often assist witnesses to manage litigation stress induced by the pressures of a legal entanglement.

Litigation consultants conduct hundreds of pre-trial focus groups and mock trials, and they speak regularly with mock jurors, and with actual jurors during post-verdict interviews. They are very knowledgeable about how jurors evaluate witnesses and the credibility of their testimony. This kind of information can be invaluable to an attorney.

To locate a trial consultant in your area, ask colleagues for recommendations or contact the American Society of Trial Consultants (www.astcweb.org). Be certain to check the consultant's education and experience to ensure the person is familiar with the type of litigation for which you are seeking assistance.

CHAPTER 11

Special Issues

Every attorney who conducts witness preparation sessions on a regular basis will eventually encounter unique or unusual situations. In our work as consultants, we continue to be amazed by the variety of circumstances under which witness preparation must be conducted. We are also often asked about the discoverability of working with a professional communications specialist or litigation psychologist. We do not have all the answers, but we can share our experiences.

Uncommon Settings

Not all witness preparation sessions can be held in an attorney's office or conference room. Sometimes the sessions must be held at the witness's place of business or home, a hotel room or hotel conference room, a hospital room, or even a jail. These locations present special problems: Will the location provide the private and confidential conditions needed? Will there be relative quiet and few interruptions? Will the witness be able to maintain focus and not be distracted by phone calls or messages? Will there be sufficient room for the attorney, the witness, and others who may be present? Will special accommodations be necessary, such as a hearing device or a video recorder?

It is always preferable to hold witness preparation sessions in the best possible setting, but if you cannot, the "make do" rule applies. It is ultimately better to hold a preparation session in a less-than-ideal setting than to avoid preparing a witness because ideal conditions cannot be arranged.

When the setting is not ideal, pre-planning is essential. Make certain the person arranging the setting (e.g., the witness, an assistant, or a facility manager) is aware of what is needed and why. For example, determine if a bed-ridden witness who is being prepared at home can arrange for a room with relative quiet. Explain the necessity of preserving the confidentiality of the proceedings by assuring that no others (i.e., family members or caregivers) will be present. Or, explain to a doctor that a hospital conference room is preferable to a cubicle office because there will be several people in attendance and surrounding noise would be very distracting.

When the Insurance Company Won't Pay for Witness Preparation

Enlightened insurers today recognize the value of pre-deposition and pre-trial witness preparation, but many continue to assume that this is a part of the attorney's responsibility for which he or she is already being paid. Unfortunately, this is not always the case. Few attorneys are experts at the kind of witness preparation outlined in this book, and few are adequately prepared to deal with a reluctant, angry, anxious, or egotistical witness. Make a case with the insurer that just as experts are needed in the case to substantiate facts and claims, an expert in witness preparation may be needed. It may be helpful to remind the insurer that the minimal dollars spent in using a litigation consultant to maximize the effectiveness of key witnesses may be repaid manyfold in a favorable verdict.

Discoverability of Witness Preparation Sessions

Preparation of one's witnesses is protected under the attorney-client privilege. The question becomes more complex when a trial consultant or litigation psychologist is called in to assist with the communication aspects of witness preparation. In a few states, it has been argued that such consultants are "experts" and thus vulnerable to the same expert discovery rules as, for example, medical experts or auto accident re-constructionists. This has been debated in other states, with the majority of rulings siding with attorney-client protections. Since trial consultants are not testifying about the facts in the case, they are not experts in the same category as professionals who can offer opinions on such topics as engineering or surgical procedures. In one state, a trial consultant was deposed in order to determine what techniques she had used to "alter" a witness. Such tactics, while extreme and misguided, are always possible.

The bottom line to the use of a trial consultant or communication expert is that most juries today are enlightened audiences who expect legal advocates to adequately prepare their witnesses. One of the authors once spoke with jurors following a verdict in a malpractice case during which the defendant doctor had been confronted on the stand during cross-examination about being prepared by a trial consultant. The doctor admitted he had needed the preparation because he had never been a witness before and felt anxious, and that he had benefited from some tips, the most important of which was to consistently tell the truth. When asked about this exchange in a post-trial interview, most of the jurors commented they expected all witnesses to be prepared by attorneys, with the help of specialized professionals, and to fail to do so likely constituted professional malpractice on the part of attorneys. So much for fearing the consequences of discovery.

While witnesses should be told the attorney will do all that is necessary to protect attorney-client privilege regarding the use of a trial consultant for pre-deposition or pre-trial preparation, it is often wiser to simply admit to doing so if pressed in cross-examination. Witnesses should be told that such preparation sessions are not secret or unethical, but are routine and customary, and an important part of the legal process.

Opposing Counsel's Inquiry into Preparation

What should a witness say if opposing counsel asks if the witness has been prepared by a non-attorney professional such as a trial consultant or litigation psychologist? Since there are variations in discovery rules across states, it is the attorney's decision about how to handle this. In states in which there is no expert discovery, this would be an inappropriate question. In other states, it is fair game. Here are some options to consider.

- Some attorneys flatly refuse to allow their witnesses to divulge such information, considering it firmly within the realm of attorney-client privilege. They argue that the consultant is part of the litigation team at the time of the preparation, under the direction of the attorney.
- Some attorneys prepare their witnesses to answer the question, in the event it is raised in a deposition or at trial. They advise their witnesses to say something like: "Yes, I was helped by a communication consultant because [see some suggestions below]."

> *"This is my first deposition/trial appearance and I was nervous. The consultant helped me understand the process and what to expect."*
>
> *"I wanted to know what to expect today so that I could respond to questions as truthfully and effectively as possible."*
>
> *"I needed to make certain I listened carefully and thought before I spoke. I wanted to make certain I was able to explain events as well as possible."*
>
> *"My attorney thought it would help me manage my nervousness."*

These responses tend to satisfy opposing counsel. However, a few attorneys may become more aggressive, in the hopes of sparking an admission that the witness was told what to say or had been "made over." More aggressive questioning might include such questions as: "Did the consultant tell you what to say?" or "Did you practice questions and answers with the consultant so you would know what to say?" or "Were you coached about what to say?"

If you anticipate this kind of questioning, it will help your witness to think through what might be an honest and appropriate response. Some examples that have actually been voiced by witnesses include:

> *"It was helpful to think through what I might be asked about, but no one told me what to say."*
>
> *"I was given an opportunity to learn what some potential questions might be and to think about how to best communicate my answers, but I was never told what to say."*
>
> *"I did not practice how to answer specific questions. I had no idea what you might ask today."*
>
> *"I doubt I could be 'made over' in the few hours we spent together. My wife hasn't been able to accomplish that in thirty years."*
>
> *"The only thing I was told was that I should speak in my own words and tell the truth. That's what I intend to do."*

Some attorneys are understandably concerned that revealing a witness has participated in a professional preparation session with a trial consultant or communication specialist will somehow "taint" the witness in the eyes of jurors. Nothing could be further from reality. Today's jurors expect witnesses to have been prepared, and they know there are professionals who specialize in it.

The lesson learned? Unless this is a battle you feel you must win, prepare your witnesses to respond to questions such as these if they are asked. The fact that a witness can handle such inquiries may prevent further questioning by opposing counsel.

It is important to assure your witness that pre-deposition or pre-trial preparation of witnesses is not only ethical, it is critical. Such assurances should be given at the beginning of the preparation session to allay any concerns on the part of the witness that what you are doing is clandestine or illegal.

APPENDIX A:

Sample Enclosure When Scheduling a Session

"What to Expect at Your Preparation Session"

Why We Are Having This Session

- To review areas of testimony we anticipate you will be questioned about at deposition or trial. This will help refresh your memory, assist you in thinking through potential responses, and reduce your anxiety about the unknown.
- To provide guidance and suggestions about how to listen to questions and how to handle difficult questions. This will help reduce your anxiety about potential "traps."
- To provide feedback to you about the effectiveness of your responses and how they are likely to be viewed by jurors and others. This will improve your confidence and credibility.
- To explain general procedures and rules. This will help you understand what to expect the day of your testimony. We will also answer any questions you may have.
- To provide guidance on your demeanor, dress, and attitude so you will make a good impression.
- To help ease your anxiety by eliminating some of the unknowns.

Who Will Be There

- Your attorney(s) will be present at the entire session. Another attorney *may* be present to role-play opposing counsel and make the practice as realistic as possible.
- A trial/communications consultant may be there to give you suggestions on how to listen to questions and give your answers most effectively, in your own words.
- Other attorneys from the firm, or other witnesses involved in the case, may be present during the session. If others will be present, your attorney will advise you.

What We Will Be Doing

- The session is for your benefit. Plan to be actively involved.
- If present, the communications consultant will want to spend a few minutes with you at the beginning of the session to get a feel for your communication style.
- We will be reviewing areas of questioning you can expect from attorneys involved in the case. If you are preparing for deposition, we will focus on cross-examination only.
- The session may be video-recorded and we may be playing back segments of tape to review your responses for content and effectiveness. This is very likely if your deposition is expected to be video-recorded by opposing counsel.

How You Should Prepare for the Session

- Review all relevant documents, as instructed by your attorney. Valuable time will be wasted if you do not know your records and documents beforehand.
- Refresh your memory about relevant events, people, and dates.
- Write out the three to six questions (or areas of questioning) about which you are most concerned, most anxious, or most uncertain about how to answer.

- Dress as you plan to dress for deposition or trial.
- Have your questions about the process in mind so they can be answered during the session.
- Get a good night's rest.
- If you expect any schedule conflicts, call your attorney immediately.

APPENDIX B:

A Basic Guide to Beginning a Witness Preparation Session

- Make an empathic statement, acknowledging that this is not a welcomed event in the person's life, but that you will use your time together efficiently and make the session as productive as possible.
- Introduce everyone present at the session and explain why they are in attendance.
- If a trial consultant or litigation psychologist is present, explain his or her role and how such a specialist can contribute to a witness's communication effectiveness.
- Tell the witness you are going to begin by reviewing the basics of the case and getting his or her perspective so that everyone's memory will be refreshed.
- Explain to the witness how both sides see the case. Be realistic.
- Point out what you see as the major strengths and challenges of both sides.
- Describe the witness's role in the case.
- Give some examples of what makes someone a good witness (eye contact, listening to the complete question, pausing, being succinct, etc.) and how you plan to work with them to improve those attributes.

- Explain what the witness is and is not responsible for—what s/he will and will not be testifying about.
- Begin the session with several witness-focused questions:
  1. What happened and what was your role in the incidents at issue? (Even if you have already gone over this, ask it again to see if anything new has been recalled.)
  2. What do you think are the weaknesses or vulnerabilities of the case?
  3. What have you been most worried about in this case? Why?
  4. How do you think you can help or hurt the case? Why?
  5. What do you most fear being asked about? Why?
  6. How much has your work and home life been affected by concerns regarding this lawsuit? Use a scale of 1 to 10, where 1 is little or no effect, and 10 is so concerned you cannot sleep well and you think or worry about it often every day.
- If the witness is a plaintiff in a civil lawsuit, ask him or her to explain and describe her injuries as s/he would describe them to a close friend or family member. Ask how those injuries have affected his or her life—work, socially, recreation, emotionally, family life, financially, etc. Emphasize the importance of being very specific, for example: "The injury to my shoulder prevents me from lifting anything heavier than a milk carton."
- If the witness is a defendant, ask for details of what the witness did, and why. Construct a timeline of critical events. Help the witness recall the thoughts and judgments that guided his or her actions at each critical point in time.

APPENDIX C:

SOME HELPFUL RESOURCES

Handbook for Witnesses: A Guide for Testifying at a Deposition, Hearing, or Trial by Angela Dodge, Ph.D. and John Ryan, Ph.D. (Print Date: May 2013). Reserve orders available by contacting adodge@dodgeconsulting.com. Purchase at www.amazon.com only after May 2013. ISBN: 978-0-9777511-9-8 ($19.95 plus S&H).

When Good Doctors Get Sued: A Practical Guide for Physicians Involved in Malpractice Lawsuits by Angela Dodge, Ph.D. in collaboration with Steven Fitzer, J.D. (Third Printing, 2009). Available by contacting adodge@dodgeconsulting.com or at www.amazon.com. ISBN: 978-09777511-0-5 ($24.95 plus S&H).

Opening Statements—Closing Arguments by Ronald J. Matlon, Ph.D. (Second Edition, 2009) Available through www.dodgepublications.com or at www.amazon.com. ISBN: 978-0-9777511-3-6 ($19.95 plus S&H).

The Expert Witness Handbook: Tips and Techniques for the Litigation Consultant by Dan Poynter (Second Edition, 1997). Available by contacting Orders@ParaPublishing.com. ISBN: 978-1568600277 ($39.95 plus S&H).

Note: Mr. Poynter uses the title "litigation consultant" to refer to expert witnesses, not psychologists who assist attorneys in preparing witnesses for deposition or trial.

Testifying in Court: Guidelines and Maxims for the Expert Witness by Stanley L. Brodsky (Eighth Printing 2001). Available through the American Psychological Association Order Department, PO Box 92984, Washington, DC 20090 or at www.amazon.com. ISBN: 978-1557985972 (price varies).

The Expert Expert Witness: More Maxims and Guidelines for Testifying in Court by Stanley L. Brodsky (Second Printing, 2003). Available through the American Psychological Association Order Department, PO Box 92984, Washington, DC 20090 or at www.amazon.com. ISBN: 978-1557985972 (price varies).

Mastering Expert Testimony: A Courtroom Handbook for Mental Health Professionals by William Tsushima and Robert Anderson Jr. (1996). Available at www.amazon.com. ISBN: 978-0805818895 (price varies).

The Psychologist as Expert Witness, Second Edition by Theodore H. Blau (2001) New York: John Wiley & Sons, Inc. Available at www.amazon.com. ISBN: 0-471-11366-2 (price varies).

Expert Witnesses in Child Abuse Cases: What Can and Should Be Said in Court by Stephen J. Ceci and Helene Hembrooke (2001). Available from American Psychological Association, Washington, DC 20090 or at www.amazon.com (price varies).

The Psychiatrist as Expert Witness, Second Edition by Thomas G. Gutheil (1998). Available through American Psychiatric Publishing, Inc. www.appi.org, Washington, DC, or at www.amazon.com. ISBN: 978-1585623426 (price varies).

Effective Expert Witnessing, Fifth Edition: Practices for the 21st Century by Jack V. Matson (2012). New York: CRC Press. Available at www.amazon.com. ISBN: 978-1-4398-8767-7 (price varies).

ABOUT THE AUTHORS

Angela M. Dodge, Ph.D. is the founding partner of Dodge Consulting and Publications LLP, a litigation consulting practice based in the Seattle-Tacoma area. An experienced trial consultant and social psychologist, she assists hundreds of attorneys across the country with witness preparation, juror-sensitive trial strategy, jury selection, pretrial research (focus groups and mock trials), and post-trial juror interviews. She has assisted in a wide range of civil cases, from personal injury and professional malpractice, to employment issues and patent infringement. Dr. Dodge has prepared several thousand witnesses, from corporate executives to hospital aides.

Her expertise in the areas of courtroom communications and jury persuasion has enabled her to consult on high-profile cases involving tobacco, breast implants, sexual abuse of children, automotive defects, environmental clean-up, police shootings, and pharmaceuticals. She has special expertise in the area of medical malpractice defense. She is the author of *When Good Doctors Get Sued: A Practical Guide for Physicians Involved in Malpractice Lawsuits* (ISBN 978-0-977751105), *Winning at Jury Selection* (ISBN 978-0-977751143), and *Handbook for Witnesses: A Guidebook for Testifying at a Deposition, Hearing, or Trial* (ISBN: 978-0-9777511-9-8). She has a solid reputation as a consultant and seminar speaker.

John H. Ryan, Ph.D. is a senior partner at Dodge Consulting and Publications LLP. Trained as a clinical psychologist, he has applied his 30+ years of experience in group and individual counseling to the practice of preparing witnesses for deposition and trial, conducting pre-trial research, and assisting with jury selection in a variety of cases. He has special expertise in litigation stress management, and has provided consultation on trial and jury selection strategy to both plaintiff and defense counsel.

Dr. Ryan has a stellar reputation for working successfully with highly anxious or otherwise challenging witnesses, and with those who are particularly intimidated by the litigation process. John has assisted in the preparation of hundreds of professionals, with emphasis on health care providers and corporate executives. In addition to this book, he is co-author of *Handbook for Witnesses: A Guide for Testifying at a Deposition, Hearing, or Trial* (ISBN: 978-0-9777511-9-8). Prior to his career as a therapist and litigation consultant, he served honorably as a USAF pilot in Vietnam, and then worked with at-risk youth as a juvenile probation officer.